BRENDA WA

PASSIONATE
Prayer
Promises

PASSIONATE

Prayer Promises

3ABN BOOKS

PO Box 220, West Frankfort, Illinois
www.3ABN.org

Pacific Press® Publishing Association
Nampa, Idaho
Oshawa, Ontario, Canada
www.PacificPress.com

Cover and interior design by Mark Bond for BONDesign, Inc.
Copyright © 2008 by Pacific Press® Publishing Association
Printed in the United States of America
All rights reserved

Library of Congress Cataloging-in-Publication Data
Walsh, Brenda, 1953-
Passionate prayer promises / Brenda Walsh with Kay Kuzma.
p. cm.
ISBN 13: 978-0-8163-2351-7
ISBN 10: 0-8163-2351-8
1. Problem solving—Religious aspects—Christianity.
2. Promises—Biblical teaching. 3. Prayer—Christianity.
4. Prayers. 5. Christian life. I. Kuzma, Kay. II. Title.
BV4599.5.P75W35 2008
242'.86—dc22
                                                        2008005992

09 10 11 12 · 5 4 3 2

DEDICATION

SPECIAL THANKS TO:

Brenda Abbott

Judy Wolter-Bailey

Phyllis Bailey

Ruth Redding Brand

Carole Derry-Bretsch

Calvin and Mary Carroll

Zina Izquerdo

Lee and Anne Jamieson

Linda Johnson

Jan Kuzma

Dave and Linda Letcher

Marie Macri

James and Bernice Micheff

Dick and Lucy Neuharth

Corky Rink

Jim and JoAnn Snelling

Dianne Wagner

Tim Walsh

Dave and Carmen Weiss

Deanna Whitehouse

Ivan and Denise Wolfe

Levi, Tyrel, and Sarah Wolfe

Prayer Topics

INTRODUCTION

rayer opens your heart to the presence, purpose, and power of God, your heavenly Father, your Savior, and your Comforter. You don't have to face your challenges or fight your battles alone. Prayer doesn't have to be flowery, loud, or long. One simple word, "Help!" can unleash tens of thousands of angels to meet whatever your need might be.

But the purpose of prayer is not just to petition God; it's also to increase your faith in His Word. Jesus prayed God's Word when He met temptation; He met each attack of Satan with, "It is written." There is power in the Word. And passionate prayer includes hanging on to God's promises. For God promises in Isaiah 55:11, that " 'my word that goes out from my mouth: It will not return to me empty, but will accomplish what I desire and achieve the purpose for which I sent it' " (NIV).

In this book you will find Bible promises that you can claim for almost every situation you may face. In addition, we have shared a prayer, using our favorite promises, and then we list additional texts for you to consider and claim. We challenge you to look up these texts, highlight them in your Bible, and refer to them often. As you do this, you'll find yourself enjoying a more passionate prayer life with our Lord and Savior and experiencing the truth of Matthew 21:22 that " 'whatever things you ask in prayer, believing, you will receive' " (NKJV). For "the LORD is faithful to all his promises and loving toward all he has made" (Psalm 145:13, NIV).

ACCEPTANCE

DEAR HEAVENLY FATHER,

More than anything, I want to be accepted for who I am, not for how I look or the things I have. Yet no matter how hard I try, I often feel like an outsider and unworthy of close relationships. It's as if I'm not as good as others and don't deserve to be accepted by them. And so I turn to You, Lord, because I know You'll never reject me. You have reminded me in Ephesians 1:3–5 that before the creation of the world You adopted me into Your family.

How special it makes me feel to be chosen by You! Oh Lord, I need You to be especially close to me today, because I'm having trouble feeling Your acceptance. I'm so thankful that my salvation is not based on feelings or good works. I'm claiming Your promise in Isaiah 41:9 that You have chosen me and not rejected me. I pray believing Your Word in 1 Samuel 12:22 that You are pleased to make me Your own.

Help me to not only feel Your acceptance but to be more accepting of others, for I know You have said in Romans 15:7 that this brings You praise. Thank You for accepting me and loving me just the way I am. In Your name—and for Your name's sake—I pray. AMEN.

Promises About Acceptance

*"Praise be to the God and Father of our Lord Jesus Christ, who…
chose us in him before the creation of the world to be holy and
blameless in his sight. In love he predestined us to be adopted as
his sons through Jesus Christ, in accordance with his pleasure
and will" (Ephesians 1:3–5, NIV).*

*" ' "You are my servant";
I have chosen you and have not rejected you' "
(Isaiah 41:9, NIV).*

*" ' For the sake of his great name the LORD will not reject his
people, because the LORD was pleased to make you his own' "
(1 Samuel 12:22, NIV).*

*"Accept one another, then, just as Christ accepted you,
in order to bring praise to God" (Romans 15:7, NIV).*

Additional Scripture and Promises

Job 3:17–19	*Luke 4:18*	*Rom. 7:6*
Ps. 119:45	*John 8:31, 32*	*1 Cor. 8:9*
Ps. 146:7	*John 8:36*	*2 Cor. 3:17*
Isa. 58:6	*Acts 7:34*	*Gal. 5:1, 13*
Isa. 61:1	*Rom. 6:6, 7, 18–22*	*1 Pet. 2:16*

ADDICTIONS

Dear Almighty God,

I'm hopelessly addicted! Please set me free from the things that are controlling my life. I've been a prisoner of my own making for too long. Lord, You know I have tried to give up my bad habits but they just hang on. Even though I cringe at what I'm doing and try to tell myself I can handle it, I feel the pull of evil and find myself yielding to my carnal nature. I just can't give up these things on my own!

Why has it taken me so long to come to the conclusion that You are the only One who has the power to live inside of me and to actually break these chains that are making me a slave to things that are hurting me—and others?

My heart and soul reaches out to claim Your promises. In Psalm 146:7, I find that, "the LORD sets prisoners free" (NIV). John 8:36 says, " 'Therefore if the Son makes you free, you shall be free indeed' " (NKJV). I also claim John 15:7, " 'If you abide in Me, and My words abide in you, you will ask what you desire, and it shall be done for you' " (NKJV). And Mark 10:27 declares, " 'With men it is impossible, but not with God; for with God all things are possible' " (NKJV). John 8:31 and 32 say that if I hold on to Your teaching, the truth will set me free!

Oh, God, Your Word is powerful. I praise You for giving me the Bible to instruct me, to convict me, to set me free from addictions, and to offer me the assurance of salvation!

I praise Your holy name. AMEN.

Promises About Addictions

"The Lord sets prisoners free"
(Psalm 146:7, NIV).

" 'Therefore if the Son makes you free, you shall be free indeed' "
(John 8:36, NKJV).

" 'If you abide in Me, and My words abide in you,
you will ask what you desire, and it shall be done for you' "
(John 15:7, NKJV).

"But Jesus looked at them and said, 'With men it is impossible,
but not with God; for with God all things are possible' "
(Mark 10:27, NKJV).

"Jesus said, 'If you hold to my teaching,
you are really my disciples. Then you will know the truth,
and the truth will set you free' "
(John 8:31, 32, NIV).

Additional Scripture and Promises

Deut. 24:5	Luke 4:18	Rom. 8:2, 21, 22
Job 3:17–19	John 8:31, 32	1 Cor. 8:9
Ps. 119:45	John 8:36	1 Cor. 9:1
Ps. 146:7	Acts 7:34	2 Cor. 3:17
Prov. 11:21	Acts 22:28	Gal. 5:1, 13
Isa. 58:6	Rom. 6:6, 7, 18-22	1 Pet. 2:16
Isa. 61:1	Rom. 7:6	

AGING

DEAR HEAVENLY FATHER,

I know my days are numbered and my life span is no longer than the width of my hand to You—as Your Word says in Psalm 39:4 and 5. But You have told me in Psalm 71:17 and 18 that even when I'm old and gray, You will not forsake me. Give me wisdom, Lord, so that I can be of a clear mind because my heart yearns to still be used by You.

My prayer is Psalm 71:9—that You will not cast me off just because I'm old, like so many tend to do with the elderly. Lord, allow me the privilege of declaring Your strength to the next generation so they will know Your power and Your love for them. In Psalm 92:12–14, You have said that the righteous will flourish like a palm tree and will bear fruit in old age. Lord, I am claiming that promise for myself.

And if it be Your will, also fulfill Your promise in Proverbs 9:11 to multiply my days and add years to my life. I ask, not for any selfish reason, but only to serve You. With every breath that is left within me, let it be used for Your honor and glory. AMEN.

PROMISES ABOUT AGING

" 'Show me, O LORD, my life's end and the number of my days;
let me know how fleeting is my life. You have made my days a
mere handbreadth; the span of my years is as nothing before you.
Each man's life is but a breath' " (Psalm 39:4, 5, NIV).

"O God, You have taught me from my youth;
And to this day I declare Your wondrous works.
Now also when I am old and grayheaded,
O God, do not forsake me,
Until I declare Your strength to this generation,
Your power to everyone who is to come"
(Psalm 71:17, 18, NKJV).

"Cast me not off in the time of old age;
forsake me not when my strength faileth" (Psalm 71:9, KJV).

"The righteous will flourish like a palm tree,…
They will still bear fruit in old age,
they will stay fresh and green" (Psalm 92:12–14, NIV).

"For by me your days will be multiplied,
And years of life will be added to you" (Proverbs 9:11, NKJV).

ADDITIONAL SCRIPTURE AND PROMISES

Deut. 5:33	*Ps. 71:17, 18*	*Eccles. 11:10*
Deut. 6:2	*Ps. 73:24–26*	*Isa. 25:8*
Job 12:12	*Ps. 90:9–14*	*Isa. 46:3, 4*
Job 19:25–27	*Prov. 3:7, 8*	*Rom. 8:38, 39*
Job 32:7, 8	*Prov. 16:31*	*Rom. 14:7, 8*
Ps. 23:4–6	*Prov. 17:6*	*2 Cor. 4:16–18*
Ps. 37:25	*Prov. 20:29*	*1 Tim. 5:1*
Ps. 48:14	*Prov. 31:30*	*1 Pet. 4:7*

ANGER

Dear Lord,

I'm really angry right now, and I'm tempted to say and do some things I shouldn't. Thank You for Your counsel in Proverbs 14:29 that it's a mistake to act impulsively. Instead, Your Word says that those who control their anger have great understanding. Lord, I need that understanding so I don't act rashly and say or do something that I'll be sorry for later. Proverbs 15:1 reminds me that harsh words will only stir up more anger!

In Nahum 1:3, You are described as slow to anger and great in power. I want to be more like You. I want to be understanding and speak softly so the problem can be resolved—but this attitude doesn't come naturally to me. So Lord, don't let me sin by allowing anger to control me as Psalm 4:4 warns. Instead, give me enough self-control to think about the situation overnight and let You fight my battles as You have promised to do in Romans 12:19.

Thank You for always being there when I need You and offering to help me through all my troubles, including the trouble I'm having right now with my anger! Amen.

Promises about Anger

"People with understanding control their anger;
a hot temper shows great foolishness"
(Proverbs 14:29, NLT).

"A soft answer turns away wrath,
But a harsh word stirs up anger" (Proverbs 15:1, NKJV).

"The Lord is slow to anger and great in power"
(Nahum 1:3, NKJV).

"Don't sin by letting anger control you.
Think about it overnight and remain silent" (Psalm 4:4, NLT).

"Beloved, do not avenge yourselves, but rather give place
to wrath; for it is written, 'Vengeance is Mine, I will repay,'
says the Lord" (Romans 12:19, NKJV).

Additional Scripture and Promises

Gen. 44:18	*Prov. 17:28*	*Rom. 12:14, 17–21*
Neh. 9:17	*Prov. 19:11*	*1 Cor. 13:5*
Ps. 37:8	*Prov. 21:19*	*Eph. 4:26, 27*
Ps. 145:8	*Prov. 22:24, 25*	*Eph. 4:31, 32*
Prov. 14:17	*Prov. 25:28*	*Col. 3:8, 21*
Prov. 15:18	*Eccles. 7:9*	*Titus 1:7*
Prov. 16:32	*Matt. 5:22–24*	*James 1:19, 20*

ANXIETY

PRECIOUS HEAVENLY FATHER,

My heart is overwhelmed with all the problems that I'm facing right now. It seems that even the smallest task stresses me out! When something goes wrong, it seems everything goes wrong. I'm so filled with anxiety that I don't have time to be thankful for—or even notice—all the blessings that You are continually bestowing on me. Forgive me, Lord, for entertaining these negative thoughts. And help me, please! I don't want to let the devil win!

Instead, I'm relying on You. In Philippians 4:6, You have counseled me not to be anxious about anything, but in everything pray and present my request to You. Lord, You know how often I come to You pleading for help, but I need to trust You more. First Peter 5:7 says that I should cast all my anxiety on You because You love me so much. In addition, I lay hold of Your promise in Isaiah 41:10: " ' "Fear not, for I am with you; Be not dismayed, for I am your God. I will strengthen you, Yes, I will help you, I will uphold you with My righteous right hand" ' " (NKJV).

So Lord, I'm giving You all my worries and anxieties. And in their place I ask that You fulfill Philippians 4:7 in my life and give me the "peace of God, which surpasses all understanding" (NKJV). Thank You for being my God and for replacing my anxieties with Your perfect peace. AMEN.

Promises About Anxiety

"Do not be anxious about anything, but in everything, by prayer and petition, with thanksgiving, present your requests to God" (Philippians 4:6, NIV).

"Cast all your anxiety on him because he cares for you" (1 Peter 5:7, NIV).

" ' "Fear not, for I am with you; Be not dismayed, for I am your God. I will strengthen you, Yes, I will help you, I will uphold you with My righteous right hand" ' " (Isaiah 41:10, NKJV).

"And the peace of God, which surpasses all understanding, will guard your hearts and minds through Christ Jesus" (Philippians 4:7, NKJV).

Additional Scripture and Promises

ASSURANCE

GRACIOUS FATHER IN HEAVEN,

This world is filled with so much sin and I can't imagine one second of my day without You in it! Thank You for the assurance of Your active involvement in my life. When trouble surrounds me, help me remember Isaiah 41:13 which reminds me that You're holding my hand. You promise in Psalm 46:1 and Isaiah 43:2, 3 that You'll even get me safely through devastating things such as floods, fire, and earthquakes, for You are my Refuge and Strength. Precious Savior, I'm so comforted by the knowledge that I never need to worry when I let You take charge of my life!

In 2 Corinthians 1:21 and 22, You tell me that You have anointed me, set Your seal of ownership on me, and put Your Spirit in my heart as a deposit, guaranteeing what is to come. I claim Your promise in Philippians 1:6 that the good work You've begun in me will be completed.

I don't even need to fear Satan, who wants so desperately to destroy me, for You, Jesus, have promised in John 10:28, 29 that You've given me eternal life and won't let anyone snatch me away. Oh thank You, Jesus! What an incredible God You are! Thank You for Your blessed assurance that You are mine, and I am Yours. AMEN.

Promises About Assurance

" 'For I, the LORD your God, will hold your right hand, Saying
to you, "Fear not, I will help you" ' " (Isaiah 41:13, NKJV).

"God is our refuge and strength, A very present help in trouble.
Therefore we will not fear, Even though the earth be removed,
And though the mountains be carried into the midst of the sea"
(Psalm 46:1, 2, NKJV).

" 'When you pass through the waters, I will be with you;
And through the rivers, they shall not overflow you.
When you walk through the fire, you shall not be burned,
Nor shall the flame scorch you.
For I am the LORD your God' " (Isaiah 43:2, 3, NKJV).

"It is God who makes both us and you stand firm in Christ. He
anointed us, set his seal of ownership on us, and put his Spirit in
our hearts as a deposit, guaranteeing what is to come"
(2 Corinthians 1:21, 22, NIV).

"[Be] confident of this, that he who began a good work in you
will carry it on to completion until the day of Christ Jesus"
(Philippians 1:6, NIV).

Additional Scripture and Promises

Deut. 33:12	Jer. 33:6	Heb. 13:6
2 Chron. 20:15	John 5:24	1 Pet. 1:3–5
Job 19:25	John 6:27, 37	1 Pet. 3:13
Ps. 9:10	John 10:28, 29	1 John 2:3
Ps. 16:5, 8	Rom. 8:37–39	1 John 3:2, 14, 19–24
Ps. 34:22	Eph. 4:30	1 John 4:6
Ps. 48:14	1 Tim. 3:13	1 John 5:2, 13–15, 18–20
Isa. 54:10	2 Tim. 1:12	Jude 24, 25

ATTITUDE

DEAR FATHER IN HEAVEN,

I know my attitude is my choice. I can choose to wallow in self-pity and bitterness, harboring negative thoughts and wasting my time criticizing, blaming, and complaining—as Satan would have me do. Or, I can choose to be like You and allow You to place upon me Your robe of righteousness. Oh Lord, make me willing to choose the attitude of Christ, described in Philippians 2:5–8, who took on the nature of a servant and humbled Himself to do His Father's will.

It is so easy to dwell on all the ugly things in my life, which make me bitter inside. But I don't want to be like that. Please give me the strength to choose a positive attitude, being content with whatever plan You have for me, just like the apostle Paul expressed in Philippians 4:11, 12: "I have learned to be content whatever the circumstances" (NKJV). Help me keep my mind on things which are true, noble, right, pure, lovely, admirable, excellent, and praiseworthy, as You would have me to do. Precious Savior, keep my mind on You and not on earthly things!

I know that I am weak and it is not possible in my sinful, human condition to always keep my thoughts focused on You. So I'm claiming Your promise in Philippians 4:13 that "I can do all things through Christ who strengthens me" (NKJV). Thank You, Jesus, for Your attitude that You are placing in my heart today and for giving me the power to be like You! AMEN.

Promises About Attitude

"Your attitude should be the same as that of Christ Jesus: Who,
being in very nature God, did not consider equality with God
something to be grasped, but made himself nothing, taking the
very nature of a servant, being made in human likeness. And
being found in appearance as a man, he humbled himself and
became obedient to death—even death on a cross!"
(Philippians 2:5–8, NIV).

"I am not saying this because I am in need, for I have learned to
be content whatever the circumstances. I know what it is to be in
need, and I know what it is to have plenty. I have learned the
secret of being content in any and every situation, whether well
fed or hungry, whether living in plenty or in want"
(Philippians 4:11, 12, NIV).

"Whatever is true, whatever is noble, whatever is right,
whatever is pure, whatever is lovely, whatever is admirable—
if anything is excellent or praiseworthy—think about such things"
(Philippians 4:8, NIV).

"I can do all things through Christ who strengthens me"
(Philippians 4:13, NKJV).

Additional Scripture and Promises

Num. 11:1	Prov. 17:22	Rom. 12:2
Deut. 30:19, 20	Lam. 3:51	Gal. 5:22, 23
Deut. 31:8	Matt. 5:8	Eph. 5:1, 2
Josh. 1:5	Matt. 6:25–30, 34	Phil. 2:5–8
Job 34:33	Matt. 23:12	Phil. 4:4–7
Ps. 77:3	Mark 7:21–23	Heb. 11:24, 25
Ps. 119:30	Luke 6:45	1 Pet. 5:6–8
Prov. 4:23	Luke 16:15	1 John 2:6

AVAILABILITY

Precious Jesus, Lord and Savior,

You are such a great and awesome God and I give all praise, honor, and glory to You. Thank You for loving me so much that You gave Your life to save me. As I get ready to live this day, I ask You to "Create in me a clean heart . . . Restore to me the joy of Your salvation," and help me to be open to Your generous Spirit, as Your Word says in Psalm 51:10 and 12.

Lord, I want my agenda to be Your agenda. Please remove all selfishness within me and make me willing to respond to Your calling like Samuel did: " ' "Speak, Lord, for Your servant hears," ' " (1 Samuel 3:9, 10, NKJV). Or, like Isaiah: " 'Here am I! Send me' " (Isaiah 6:8, NKJV). Use me, Lord. I'm available! Second Chronicles 31:21 records that in everything Hezekiah undertook "he sought his God and worked wholeheartedly. And so he prospered" (NIV). I want to be like that!

I love Your promise in Hebrews 6:10: "God is not unjust; he will not forget your work and the love you have shown him as you have helped his people and continue to help them" (NIV). Oh heavenly Father, today I want to walk worthy of the calling You have given me—and to share Your love with others. I want to always be available to You! In Your name I pray. Amen.

Promises About Availability

"Create in me a clean heart, O God, And renew a steadfast spirit within me. . . . Restore to me the joy of Your salvation, And uphold me by Your generous Spirit" (Psalm 51:10, 12, NKJV).

"Samuel went and lay down in his place. The LORD came and stood there, calling as at the other times, 'Samuel! Samuel!' Then Samuel said, 'Speak, for your servant is listening' " (1 Samuel 3:9, 10, NIV).

"Then I heard the voice of the LORD saying, 'Whom shall I send? And who will go for us?' And I said, 'Here am I. Send me!' " (Isaiah 6:8, NIV).

"In everything that [Hezekiah] undertook in the service of God's temple and in obedience to the law and the commands, he sought his God and worked wholeheartedly. And so he prospered" (2 Chronicles 31:21, NIV).

"God is not unjust; he will not forget your work and the love you have shown him as you have helped his people and continue to help them" (Hebrews 6:10, NIV).

Additional Scripture and Promises

Deut. 6:13	Ps. 63:3	Rom. 12:1, 2, 10–13
Deut. 10:12	Ps. 100:1–4	Eph. 4:1, 2
Deut. 13:4	Isa. 50:4, 5	1 Cor. 3:9
Josh. 22:5	Matt. 24:44–47	2 Cor. 5:20
Josh. 24:15	Mark 1:16, 18	2 Cor. 8:11, 12
1 Sam. 7:3	Luke 1:30, 31, 38	Gal. 5:13
1 Sam. 12:20–22, 24	John 12:26	Eph. 6:7
1 Chron. 28:9	Rom. 7:6	Col. 3:23

BELIEVING
GOD'S PROMISES

Dear God of the Universe,

Your Word is full of promises. On almost every page I find something to give me hope and courage to help me through my day. Thank You, Lord, for reminding me that You have always stood behind Your Word! I love how You told Moses in Numbers 11:23 that You can work the same miracles today as You did in the past—that Your arm has not been shortened! What an awesome and powerful God You are!

You have demonstrated time and time again that You always keep Your promises. In Psalm 89:34 You said, "My covenant [with David] I will not break, Nor alter the word that has gone out of My lips" (NKJV). You told Isaiah in Isaiah 46:11, " 'I have spoken it; I will also bring it to pass' " (NKJV). And to Ezekiel in Ezekiel 36:36 you promised, " 'I the LORD, have spoken it, and I will do it' " (NKJV).

The evidence is overwhelming! You, Oh Lord, are 100 percent faithful! That's why I believe Your words in John 14:14, that if I ask anything in Your name, You will do it! I praise Your holy name and believe in Your promises! AMEN.

Promises About Believing God's Promises

"And the LORD said to Moses, 'Has the LORD's arm been shortened? Now you shall see whether what I say will happen to you or not'" (Numbers 11:23, NKJV).

"My covenant I will not break, Nor alter the word that has gone out of My lips. Once I have sworn by My holiness; I will not lie to David: His seed shall endure forever, And his throne as the sun before Me" (Psalm 89:34–36, NKJV).

" 'Indeed I have spoken it; I will also bring it to pass. I have purposed it; I will also do it' " (Isaiah 46:11, NKJV).

" 'Then the nations which are left all around you shall know that I, the LORD, have rebuilt the ruined places and planted what was desolate. I, the LORD, have spoken it, and I will do it' " (Ezekiel 36:36, NKJV).

" 'If you ask anything in My name, I will do it' " (John 14:14, NKJV).

Additional Scripture and Promises

Gen. 18:14	Jer. 33:14	Gal. 3:29
Num. 23:19, 20	Ezek. 24:14	1 Thess. 5:24
Josh. 1:5	Matt. 19:26	Titus 1:1, 2
1 Kings 8:56	Matt. 24:35	Heb. 9:15
Ps. 31:19	Mark 9:23	Heb. 10:23, 36
Ps. 37:4	John 14:13	2 Pet. 1:4
Ps. 77:8	Rom. 4:20, 21	2 Pet. 3:9
Ps. 145:16	1 Cor. 10:13	

BLESSINGS

DEAR FATHER IN HEAVEN,

I long in my heart for the blessings and abundant life that only You can give. I want my heart to be pure so that You can use me to bring others closer to You. I plead earnestly with You as Jacob did so long ago—recorded in Genesis 32:24–29—for You to bless me. Please keep me close to You and give me the strength and courage to keep Your commandments so that I may receive the blessing You have promised me in Deuteronomy 11:26, 27.

I pray the prayer of Jabez in 1 Chronicles 4:10 and ask You to expand my territory, keep Your hand upon me, and keep me from evil. Lord, I long to have a oneness with You and experience the blessings that You have promised in Numbers 6:24–26 that You will shine Your face upon me, be gracious unto me, and give me peace!

You are such an awesome God, and I praise You for Your goodness and mercy! Thank You for loving me and giving me the assurance in Psalm 2:12 that I have only to put my trust in You and You will bless me. Lord, I am trusting in You, my precious Savior, and I am thanking You in advance for what I know You are about to do! AMEN.

Promises About Blessings

"Then Jacob was left alone; and a Man wrestled with him until the breaking of day. . . . And He said, 'Let Me go, for the day breaks.' But he [Jacob] said, 'I will not let You go unless You bless me!' . . . And He blessed him there"
(Genesis 32:24–29, NKJV).

"I am setting before you today a blessing . . . if you obey the commands of the LORD your God that I am giving you today"
(Deuteronomy 11:26, 27, NIV).

" 'Oh, that You would bless me indeed, and enlarge my territory, that Your hand would be with me, and that You would keep me from evil' " (1 Chronicles 4:10, NKJV).

" 'The LORD bless you and keep you;
The LORD make His face shine upon you,
And be gracious to you;
The LORD lift up His countenance upon you,
And give you peace' " (Numbers 6:24–26, NKJV).

"Blessed are all they that put their trust in him"
(Psalm 2:12, KJV).

Additional Scripture and Promises

Gen. 12:2, 3	*Ps. 67:1, 7*	*Prov. 14:21*
Num. 6:24–26	*Ps. 84:5*	*Isa. 30:18*
Deut. 11:26, 27	*Ps. 89:15*	*Isa. 56:2*
Ps. 5:12	*Ps. 94:12*	*Matt. 5:3–11*
Ps. 23:5, 6	*Ps. 112:1, 2*	*Luke 6:20–23*
Ps. 31:19	*Ps. 119:1, 2*	*Luke 14:13, 14*
Ps. 32:1, 2	*Ps. 128:1–6*	*Rom. 4:7*
Ps. 41:1	*Prov. 3:33*	*Rom. 10:12, 13*

CHOICES

DEAR CREATOR GOD,

I come before You asking for Your help. There are so many decisions to make, and I need direction from You that I may make the right choices! I love You so much for giving us the gift of choice. It's one of the greatest gifts You could have ever given us. But I confess that I don't always make good choices. Sometimes I have chosen to spend time with others, rather than spending time with You. And sometimes I have chosen to indulge in habits that dull my mind to the precious impressions of Your Holy Spirit, rather than exercise self-denial.

Oh Lord, forgive me. I know You are a jealous God— You want to be the only God in my life. Before I impulsively make decisions, help me to give careful thought to my ways, as Haggai 1:5 says I should do. I want to follow Your instruction in Proverbs 8:10 and 11 to choose Your instruction, Your knowledge, and Your wisdom rather than silver, gold, or rubies.

I claim the promise in Proverbs 16:9, that although I make plans, You will determine my steps. And even when I fail, thank You for reminding me in John 15:16 that You have chosen me—and that no choice I make will ever change that fact. Thank You, in Jesus' name. AMEN.

PROMISES ABOUT CHOICES

"This is what the LORD Almighty says:
'Give careful thought to your ways' " (Haggai 1:5, NIV).

"Choose my instruction instead of silver, knowledge rather
than choice gold, for wisdom is more precious than rubies,
and nothing you desire can compare with her"
(Proverbs 8:10, 11, NIV).

"In his heart a man plans his course,
but the LORD determines his steps" (Proverbs 16:9, NIV).

" 'You did not choose Me, but I chose you and appointed you
that you should go and bear fruit, and that your fruit should
remain, that whatever you ask the Father in My name
He may give you' " (John 15:16, NKJV).

ADDITIONAL SCRIPTURE AND PROMISES

Gen. 13:11
Exod. 32:26
Deut. 12:8
Deut. 30:15, 19, 20
1 Kings 18:21
Job 34:33
Ps. 20:4
Ps. 37:4–6

Ps. 65:4
Ps. 119:30–35
Prov. 1:29
Prov. 3:5, 6, 21–23
Prov. 8:10–12, 14–21
Prov. 12:15
Prov. 14:22
Prov. 16:3, 9

Prov. 22:1
Dan. 1:8
Dan. 3:18
Matt. 6:24
Matt. 7:13, 14
Acts 9:15
1 Cor. 1:27
Heb. 11:24, 25

CHURCH FELLOWSHIP

DEAR HOLY GOD,

There seems to be so many hypocrites in my church and so many egos. I get discouraged with all the politics. Is it really important to You that I go to church? After all, can't I worship You in the peace and comfort of my own home?

But then I am reminded of what Jesus said in Matthew 18:20, "Where two or three come together in my name, there am I with them" (NIV). And Hebrews 10:25 says we should not neglect meeting together because we need each other. Something special happens when believers worship together!

You have said in Romans 12:4–6 that Christ's body (the church) needs to be like a human body that has different functioning parts all working together. Psalm 133:1 says, "Behold, how good and how pleasant it is for brethren to dwell together in unity!" (NKJV). I want that for my church!

Oh Lord, help me follow Your command in 1 Peter 3:8, 9 to "Live in harmony with one another; be sympathetic, love as brothers, be compassionate and humble. Do not repay evil with evil or insult with insult, but with blessing, because to this you were called so that you may inherit a blessing" (NIV). Lord, I claim that blessing for me—and my church! Help me to not look at others, but only to You. And whatever changes need to be made, Lord, let them begin with me! AMEN.

PROMISES ABOUT CHURCH FELLOWSHIP

" 'For where two or three come together in my name,
there am I with them' " (Matthew 18:20, NIV).

"And let us not neglect our meeting together, as some people do, but
encourage one another, especially now that the day of his return is
drawing near" (Hebrews 10:25, NLT).

"Just as each of us has one body with many members,
and these members do not all have the same function,
so in Christ we who are many form one body, and each
member belongs to all the others" (Romans 12:4, 5, NIV).

"Behold, how good and how pleasant it is for brethren
to dwell together in unity!" (Psalm 133:1, NKJV).

"Finally, all of you, live in harmony with one another;
be sympathetic, love as brothers, be compassionate and humble.
Do not repay evil with evil or insult with insult, but with
blessing, because to this you were called so that you
may inherit a blessing" (1 Peter 3:8, 9, NIV).

ADDITIONAL SCRIPTURE AND PROMISES

Ps. 84:4, 7	Matt. 6:33	Phil. 2:1–4
Ps. 89:7	Acts 1:14	Col. 1:13, 18
Ps. 92:13, 14	Acts 2:41–47	Col. 2:10, 19
Ps. 111:1	Acts 11: 26	Col. 3:16
Ps. 122:1	1 Cor. 1:9	1 Tim. 3:15
Ps. 133	1 Cor. 12:12–20, 25–28	1 Pet. 2:9
Zeph. 2:10	Eph. 2:19–22	1 John 1:1–7
Mal. 3:16	Phil. 1:3–6	Rev. 3:20

COMFORT

DEAR LOVING FATHER IN HEAVEN,

My heart is aching with sadness and the pain deep within me is overwhelming. Lord, You know me better than anyone, and You alone can help me. I claim Your promise in Isaiah 57:15 that You are with the contrite—those who are broken and crushed. Oh Father, that's me! Please take me in Your arms and hold me close to Your heart as the shepherd holds his sheep in Isaiah 40:11.

My eyes are so blinded by my tears that I can't see the light at the end of the tunnel. I don't know what I would do without You in my life. Thank You for Your promise that although I now have sorrow, my heart will once again rejoice, and no one will be able to take my joy away.

What an affirmation of Your love for me in Psalm 56:8 where You want me to remember that You keep track of all my sorrows! I am not going through this alone! Restore my life and increase my honor, as You've promised in Psalm 71:19–21.

Precious Father, when I am weak and forgetful please continue to remind me that this heartbreaking time is only for a season! Help me to hang on to Your promise in Jeremiah 31:13 that You " 'will turn [my] mourning into gladness; [and] will give [me] comfort and joy instead of sorrow' " (NIV). Oh, dear God, please give me the strength to reach out and accept Your gift of comfort and joy You have for me today! AMEN.

PROMISES ABOUT COMFORT

"For thus says the High and Lofty One Who inhabits eternity, whose name is Holy: 'I dwell in the high and holy place, With him who has a contrite [crushed] and humble spirit, To revive the spirit of the humble, And to revive the heart of the contrite ones'"
(Isaiah 57:15, NKJV).

"[The LORD] tends his flock like a shepherd: He gathers the lambs in his arms and carries them close to his heart; he gently leads those that have young" (Isaiah 40:11, NIV).

*"You keep track of all my sorrows.
You have collected all my tears in your bottle.
You have recorded each one in your book" (Psalm 56:8, NLT).*

"Who, O God, is like you? Though you have made me see troubles, many and bitter, you will restore my life again; from the depths of the earth you will again bring me up. You will increase my honor and comfort me once again" (Psalm 71:19–21, NIV).

*"'I will turn their mourning into gladness; I will give them comfort and joy instead of sorrow' . . . declares the LORD"
(Jeremiah 31:13, 14, NIV).*

ADDITIONAL SCRIPTURE AND PROMISES

Deut. 33:12	Ps. 37:24, 39	Nahum 1:7
Num. 6:24–26	Ps. 94:18, 19	Zeph. 3:17
Josh. 1:5, 9	Ps. 119:49, 50, 52, 76	Matt. 5:1, 2, 4
Ps. 9:9	Ps. 147:3	Matt. 9:22
Ps. 18:2	Isa. 12:1	Matt. 11:28
Ps. 23:4	Isa. 30:19	John 14:1, 16, 18
Ps. 27:14	Lam. 3:31-33	John 16:20–33
Ps. 34:18	Jer. 15:15	2 Cor. 1:3–5

COMMANDMENTS

DEAR GOD IN HEAVEN,

I know I should keep all of Your Ten Commandments holy. But I am struggling. I realize how important it is for me to obey them because You have told me in Ecclesiastes 12:13 to "Fear God and keep his commandments, for this is the whole duty of man" (NIV). I know that I am not saved by works; but I am to serve You to show my love for You. For in John 14:15 You tell me, " 'If you love Me, keep My commandments' " (NKJV).

Oh Lord, I love You so much! However, there are so many temptations all around me—and I am weak. Please give me the strength and courage to keep Your commandments. I want to show You how very much I love You. I also want to abide in Your love as You have promised me in John 15:10: " 'If you keep My commandments, you will abide in My love' " (NKJV). I realize that You gave Your commandments so I could have a better life, and that following them is for my own good. So I'm claiming Deuteronomy 4:40 where You promise that if I keep Your commandments, it will go well with me and with my children after me, and that You will prolong my days on the earth.

Lord, please prolong my life that I may spend every minute living as You have commanded and giving You praise, honor, and glory! In Your holy name I pray. AMEN.

Promises About the Commandments

"Fear God and keep his commandments, for this is the whole duty of man" (Ecclesiastes 12:13, NIV).

" 'If you love Me, keep My commandments' " (John 14:15, NKJV).

" 'If you keep My commandments, you will abide in My love, just as I have kept My Father's commandments and abide in His love' " (John 15:10, NKJV).

"Thou shalt keep therefore his statutes, and his commandments, which I command thee this day, that it may go well with thee, and with thy children after thee, and that thou mayest prolong thy days upon the earth, which the LORD thy God giveth thee, for ever" (Deuteronomy 4:40, KJV).

Additional Scripture and Promises

Gen. 26:5	*Ps. 19:8–11*	*John 14:15*
Exod. 31:18	*Ps. 103:17, 18*	*Rom. 7:12*
Deut. 4:2, 13, 40	*Prov. 3:1-4*	*Eph. 6:2*
Deut. 7:9	*Prov. 6:22, 23*	*1 Tim. 1:5*
Deut. 10:12, 13	*Eccles. 12:13*	*1 John 2:3–11*
Deut. 11:26–28	*Ezek. 11:19, 20*	*2 John 6*
Josh. 22:5	*Matt. 15:3–6*	*Rev. 12:17*
1 Kings 8:57, 58	*Matt. 22:40*	*Rev. 22:14*
2 Chron. 24:20	*Mark 10:19*	

COMPANIONSHIP

Dear Heavenly Father,

I'm so thankful I can approach Your throne room anytime, day or night. You are never too busy for me; no topic is too trivial to bring to You. I know this isn't a life-or-death situation, but Lord, I've come to ask for a companion with whom I can share my life's journey. Even You said in Genesis 2:18 that it isn't good for man to be alone—and then You created Eve for Adam.

I don't know why I'm still single, but I know that if it is in Your plan for me to have a mate, You will find me one! So I'm claiming Psalm 37:4 and 5, that if I delight myself in You, You'll give me the desires of my heart. And if I commit myself to You and trust in You, You will bring it to pass. What a beautiful promise! But Lord, if having a special companion is not in Your plans for me, that's OK. I wish it hadn't taken me so long to realize that You are all I need!

Please put Your love in my heart for others, so that I can have the love you talk about in 1 John 3:11. I claim the promise in 1 John 4:12 that says, "If we love one another, God abides in us, and His love has been perfected in us" (NKJV). Precious Father, please perfect Your love in me. Help me to let all I do be done in love, as You have instructed in 1 Corinthians 16:14, that I might bring joy to Your heart. Amen.

PROMISES ABOUT COMPANIONSHIP

*"And the LORD God said, 'It is not good that man should be alone; I will make him a helper comparable to him' "
(Genesis 2:18, NKJV).*

"Delight yourself also in the LORD, And He shall give you the desires of your heart. Commit your way to the LORD, Trust also in Him, And He shall bring it to pass" (Psalm 37:4, 5, NKJV).

"For this is the message that you heard from the beginning, that we should love one another" (1 John 3:11, NKJV).

*"No one has seen God at any time. If we love one another, God abides in us, and His love has been perfected in us"
(1 John 4:12, NKJV).*

*"Let all that you do be done with love"
(1 Corinthians 16:14, NKJV).*

ADDITIONAL SCRIPTURE AND PROMISES

Gen. 2:24	*Eccles. 4:9–12*	*2 Cor. 6:14*
Prov. 1:15, 16	*Song of Sol. 8:2*	*Eph. 4:2, 3*
Prov. 3:3-6	*Isa. 54:5*	*Phil. 2:1, 2*
Prov. 13:20	*Isa. 62:5*	*Col. 2:2, 3*
Prov. 17:17	*Hosea 2:19, 20*	*1 Pet. 3:8*
Prov. 18:22–24	*Amos 3:3*	*1 Pet. 4:8*
Prov. 22:24, 25	*John 15:12, 13*	
Prov. 27:9	*Rom. 12:10*	

COMPLAINING

Dear Lord and Savior,

Help me to be a person who is satisfied with the blessings that You give me, as Hebrews 13:5 tells me I should be. So often I find myself complaining about my job, my family, my spouse—basically about everything in my life. I don't know why I am always so negative. Lord, please change me to be like the apostle Paul who describes himself in Philippians 4:11 as having learned to be content no matter what his situation might be.

I don't know why I continue to find fault with not only myself, but others as well. Nothing is ever good enough, and I feel so unhappy inside. Please fill me with a stronger desire to walk with You that I may reflect Your character within me. I know how strongly You feel about complaining, for in Numbers 11:1 You have said that when the people complained, it displeased You. And in Philippians 2:14 You instruct me to "Do all things without complaining and disputing" (NKJV).

Help me to be a person who speaks kindly and politely, one who is sensitive to the feelings of others. May the words of my mouth cease to complain and only bring You praise. Amen.

Promises About Complaining

"Let your conduct be without covetousness; be content with such things as you have. For He Himself has said, 'I will never leave you nor forsake you' " (Hebrews 13:5, NKJV).

"Not that I speak in regard to need, for I have learned in whatever state I am, to be content" (Philippians 4:11, NKJV).

"Now when the people complained, it displeased the Lord; for the Lord heard it, and His anger was aroused. So the fire of the Lord burned among them, and consumed some in the outskirts of the camp" (Numbers 11:1, NKJV).

"Do all things without complaining and disputing, that you may become blameless and harmless, children of God without fault in the midst of a crooked and perverse generation, among whom you shine as lights in the world" (Philippians 2:14, 15, NKJV).

Additional Scripture and Promises

Deut. 12:7	*Eccles. 4:6, 8*	*Phil. 4:11*
Job 9:27	*Jer. 31:14*	*1 Tim. 6:6–8*
Ps. 37:1, 7	*Lam. 3:39*	*Jude 16*
Ps. 144:14, 15	*Phil. 2:14, 15*	

CONDEMNATION

DEAR HEAVENLY FATHER,

I come to You seeking comfort that only You can give. It seems everyone has turned against me and treats me as an outcast just for worshiping You. Even people that I love have shunned me. I have no way to defend myself as they will not listen, yet the sting of condemnation hurts so deeply.

Oh Lord, You know everything and truly understand my heart. I am ridiculed for going to church, and yet the only joy in my life is spending time with You. I am clinging to Your promise in 1 Peter 3:14 that You will bless me and will encourage me not to be afraid. You tell me in 1 Peter 4:14 and 16 that if I suffer for being a Christian I should not be ashamed, and that it is a blessing to suffer for You.

Please let my life glorify You! Even though people say hurtful things and turn their backs on me, give me love in my heart for them. Let me feed them when they are hungry and give them water to drink when they are thirsty as You have admonished me to do in Romans 12:19–21. Most of all, precious Father, keep me faithful and close to You. In Your name I pray. AMEN.

PROMISES ABOUT CONDEMNATION

"But even if you should suffer for righteousness' sake, you are blessed. 'And do not be afraid of their threats, nor be troubled'" (1 Peter 3:14, NKJV).

"If you are reproached for the name of Christ, blessed are you, for the Spirit of glory and of God rests upon you. On their part He is blasphemed, but on your part He is glorified. . . . Yet if anyone suffers as a Christian, let him not be ashamed, but let him glorify God in this matter" (1 Peter 4:14, 16, NKJV).

"Do not take revenge, my friends, but leave room for God's wrath, for it is written: 'It is mine to avenge; I will repay,' says the Lord. On the contrary: 'If your enemy is hungry, feed him; if he is thirsty, give him something to drink. In doing this, you will heap burning coals on his head.' Do not be overcome by evil, but overcome evil with good" (Romans 12:19–21, NIV).

ADDITIONAL SCRIPTURE AND PROMISES

Ps. 37:8	Prov. 25:21, 22	Eph. 4:26, 31, 32
Prov. 15:1, 18	Luke 6:22, 23	Col. 3:21
Prov. 19:11	John 15:18-21	1 Pet. 3:14–16
Prov. 22:24, 25	Rom. 5:1, 2	

CONFLICT

DEAR PRECIOUS FATHER,

Thank You for being my Lord and Savior, for I can't imagine my life without You in it! I long to be more like You, and yet I fail so miserably. I struggle with having Your sweet Spirit within me that You describe in Ephesians 4:3. Sometimes I can get so irritated with others that my actions are not always Christlike.

And yet, You have told me in Philippians 2:14–16 to do everything without complaining or arguing so that I can shine out like the "stars in the universe" and hold up God's Word. And in Ecclesiastes 7:9 You admonish me not to be quickly provoked. Please keep my tongue from saying hurtful things or lashing out, even if it is justified. Sometimes sharp words just come out of my mouth before I can stop them! Lord, I don't want to be the fool You talk about in Proverbs 20:3, who is quick to quarrel. Instead, I want to avoid strife.

I want others to see You in me. And You never spoke impulsively, hurting other's feelings and justifying Yourself in such a way as to cause conflict. Instead, Isaiah 53:7 describes You as being oppressed and afflicted, yet not opening Your mouth.

I claim Your promise in Psalm 86:7 to answer me in my time of trouble. Help me, Father God, to avoid conflict by always having Your sweet Spirit within me! In the name of Jesus I pray. AMEN.

PROMISES ABOUT CONFLICT

"Make every effort to keep the unity of the Spirit through the bond of peace" (Ephesians 4:3, NIV).

"Do everything without complaining or arguing, so that you may become blameless and pure, children of God without fault in a crooked and depraved generation, in which you shine like stars in the universe as you hold out the word of life—in order that I may boast on the day of Christ that I did not run or labor for nothing" (Philippians 2:14–16, NIV).

"Do not be quickly provoked in your spirit" (Ecclesiastes 7:9, NIV).

"It is to a man's honor to avoid strife, but every fool is quick to quarrel" (Proverbs 20:3, NIV).

"He was oppressed and He was afflicted, Yet He opened not His mouth" (Isaiah 53:7, NKJV).

"In the day of my trouble I will call upon You, For You will answer me" (Psalm 86:7, NKJV).

ADDITIONAL SCRIPTURE AND PROMISES

Ps. 55:18	Prov. 24:17–20	1 Cor. 1:10
Ps. 86:7	Prov. 29:22	1 Cor. 12:25, 26
Prov. 12:16	Eccles. 7:9	Eph. 4:3, 26, 31, 32
Prov. 15:1, 18	Matt. 5:22	Phil. 2:14–16
Prov. 19:11	John 15:18–21	Col. 3:21
Prov. 20:3	John 17:1, 20, 23	2 Thess. 3:3
Prov. 21:19	Rom. 5:1, 2	1 Pet. 3:14
Prov. 22:24, 25	Rom. 12:17–21	1 Pet. 4:14, 16

CONFUSION

DEAR ALMIGHTY GOD,

I'm stumbling along like a lost sheep in the wilderness. I don't know what to do. One minute I think one way, and the next another. You know what I need because You are my Shepherd (Psalm 23:1). I pray the prayer of David in Psalm 139:23 and 24, "Search me, O God, and know my heart; Try me, and know my anxieties; And see if there is any wicked way in me" (NKJV). Precious Father, I don't want any selfish desires to keep me from following Your plan for my life.

Make the status of my spiritual condition clear to me so my parched soul can become the watered garden You promise in Isaiah 58:11. In Isaiah 42:16 You say You'll lead the blind in new places and make the darkness light and the crooked places straight. Oh Lord, I need You to do this for me. I claim Your promise in Psalm 37:23 and 24 that even though I'm stumbling now, You'll make my steps firm and keep me from falling.

My deepest desire is to follow the path You have chosen for me, so please give me wisdom and discernment. Erase all confusion and make Your ways plain and clear. In Your Holy name I pray. AMEN.

Promises About Confusion

"The LORD is my shepherd; I shall not want"
(Psalm 23:1, NKJV).

"Search me, O God, and know my heart;
Try me, and know my anxieties;
And see if there is any wicked way in me,
And lead me in the way everlasting"
(Psalm 139:23, 24, NKJV).

" 'The LORD will guide you continually,
And satisfy your soul in drought,
And strengthen your bones;
You shall be like a watered garden,
And like a spring of water, whose waters do not fail' "
(Isaiah 58:11, NKJV).

" 'I will bring the blind by a way they did not know;
I will lead them in paths they have not known.
I will make darkness light before them,
And crooked places straight. These things I will do for them,
And not forsake them' " (Isaiah 42:16, NKJV).

"If the LORD delights in a man's way, he makes his steps firm;
though he stumble, he will not fall, for the LORD
upholds him with his hand" (Psalm 37:23, 24, NIV).

Additional Scripture and Promises

Ps. 17:5–8	*Isa. 26:3*	*Rev. 1:3*
Ps. 63:7, 8	*Mark 4:39*	*Rev. 19:9*
Ps. 119:28, 105	*Rom. 5:1*	*Rev. 22:7, 14*
Prov. 14:12	*Phil. 2:5*	
Prov. 16:3	*James 1:12, 17*	

CONTENTMENT

DEAR LORD, MY SAVIOR AND FRIEND,

You know me better than anyone else, and yet I am amazed that You still love me! I don't understand how that is possible when You see how I struggle with never being satisfied with the blessings that You have given me in my life.

You have told me in Hebrews 13:5 to be content with the things that I have, but that is so hard for me to do. Everyone I know seems to have a better car, a better house, better clothes, better kids, a better spouse and, in general, a better life! Teach me, Lord, the secret that Paul expressed in Philippians 4:11–13 of being able to be content in every situation. I claim Proverbs 19:23—Your promise that the fear of the Lord will lead my life and that I will be content, untouched by trouble! For You have told me in 1 Timothy 6:6 that godliness with contentment is great gain!

Oh precious Father, I want Your godliness within me! Help me to appreciate the many blessings in my life, starting with You—my awesome and mighty God! AMEN.

Promises About Contentment

"Let your conduct be without covetousness; be content with such things as you have. For He Himself has said, 'I will never leave you nor forsake you'" (Hebrews 13:5, NKJV).

"I am not saying this because I am in need, for I have learned to be content whatever the circumstances. I know what it is to be in need, and I know what it is to have plenty. I have learned the secret of being content in any and every situation, whether well fed or hungry, whether living in plenty or in want. I can do everything through him who gives me strength" (Philippians 4:11–13, NIV).

"The fear of the Lord leads to life: Then one rests content, untouched by trouble" (Proverbs 19:23, NIV).

"Now godliness with contentment is great gain" (1 Timothy 6:6, NKJV).

Additional Scripture and Promises

Deut. 12:7
Josh. 7:7
Job 1:21
Ps. 37:16, 17
Ps. 144:14, 15
Prov. 12:14

Prov. 14:30
Prov. 15:15
Prov. 17:22
Prov. 19:23
Prov. 23:17, 18
Eccles. 4:6

Eccles. 5:10
Isa. 26:3
Jer. 31:14
Mark 15:15
1 Tim. 6:6–8

COURAGE &
CONFIDENCE

Dear Almighty God,

I stand in awe of Your greatness and long for the confidence that only You can give. It seems that no matter how hard I try, I just can't seem to do things as well as others. I know that You have given me many talents, but I lack the courage to step out of my comfort zone and use them. And yet, I long to be a soul-winning tool for You. So I am asking You to fill me with Your courage.

As Jeremiah 32:17 declares, " ' "Ah, Lord God! Behold, . . . There is nothing too hard for You" ' " (NKJV). And Job 42:1, 2 tells me, " 'I know that You [Lord] can do everything' " (NKJV). You even gave Your disciples authority to trample on snakes and scorpions and to overcome the power of the enemy (Luke 10:19). I'm asking for that same kind of power. You know what I'm facing and that I'm feeling inadequate. In fact, I'm downright scared!

Thank You for reminding me in 2 Chronicles 20:15 that the battle is Yours—not mine. I am empowered by Your words in Deuteronomy 31:6 that I should be " 'strong and courageous . . . for the Lord your God goes with you; he will never leave you nor forsake you' "(NIV). Wow! What a promise! Thank You, Lord, for always being with me. With You by my side, I never need to fear!

Heavenly Father, please replace all my feelings of intimidation and inadequacy with Your courage and confidence. May I go forward with holy boldness! I place all my faith and trust in You. In Your holy name I pray. Amen.

Promises About Courage & Confidence

" ' "Ah, Lord God! Behold, You have made the heavens and the earth by Your great power and outstretched arm. There is nothing too hard for You" ' " (Jeremiah 32:17, NKJV).

"Then Job answered the Lord and said: 'I know that You can do everything, And that no purpose of Yours can be withheld from You' " (Job 42:1, 2, NKJV).

" 'Thus says the Lord to you: "Do not be afraid nor dismayed because of this great multitude, for the battle is not yours, but God's" ' " (2 Chronicles 20:15, NKJV).

Moses said, " 'Be strong and courageous. Do not be afraid or terrified . . . for the Lord your God goes with you; he will never leave you nor forsake you' " (Deuteronomy 31:6, NIV).

Additional Scripture and Promises

CRITICISM

HEAVENLY FATHER,

I became painfully aware of my sin of criticism when I read Your words in Luke 6:37 that I am not to judge or to condemn, but rather to forgive—and that if I don't, then I will be treated the same way I have treated others. Lord, I'm ashamed at what I have said to others—or about others. I'm hurt when people are critical of me, so I'm sure my words have hurt them as well. I'm so sorry!

I just expect people to do things my way, and if they don't measure up, I have this terrible habit of pointing it out. I have been further rebuked by 1 Thessalonians 4:11 that tells me I should aspire to lead a quiet life and mind my own business. Wow! I realize that I'm caught in a dangerous rut and need Your help to change my ways to become the person You want me to be. In John 3:17 You have said, " 'For God did not send His Son into the world to condemn the world, but that the world through Him might be saved' " (NKJV).

Thank You for saving me and not condemning me. Please forgive me for my unloving and critical spirit. With Your help, my desire is to follow the admonition in Philippians 3:14 to press toward the goal for the prize of the upward call of God in Christ Jesus. With thanksgiving I claim all that You have promised me in Jesus' name. AMEN.

Promises About Criticism

" 'Judge not, and you shall not be judged. Condemn not, and you shall not be condemned. Forgive, and you will be forgiven' " (Luke 6:37, NKJV).

"That you also aspire to lead a quiet life, to mind your own business, and to work with your own hands, as we commanded you" (1 Thessalonians 4:11, NKJV).

" 'For God did not send His Son into the world to condemn the world, but that the world through Him might be saved' " (John 3:17, NKJV).

"I press toward the goal for the prize of the upward call of God in Christ Jesus" (Philippians 3:14, NKJV).

Additional Scripture and Promises

Exod. 20:16
Exod. 23:1, 7
Lev. 19:16
Ps. 15:1–3
Ps. 37:1
Prov. 19:9
Prov. 26:27
Zech. 7:10

Matt. 7:3–5
Matt. 12:36
Matt. 18:15
Matt. 27:12
Luke 3:14
Acts 23:5
Rom. 2:1
1 Cor. 2:11

1 Cor. 13:4, 5
Gal. 6:4
1 Timothy 5:19
Titus 3:2
James 1:26
James 4:11

DEALING
WITH PARENTS

DEAR JESUS,

You were a child at one time and had to deal with Your parents—just as I have to now. I sometimes get frustrated at the way my folks treat me, but I try hard to listen to them as the Bible tells me to do in Proverbs 1:8. And I try to treat my parents as You did Yours. I read in Luke 2:46–50 about Your mom and dad leaving You in Jerusalem when You were twelve, and then Your mom blaming You. I think I would have set the record straight and told her it was really her fault, but You didn't hurt her feelings. Instead, You calmly explained the reason You were at the temple.

Then in John 2:1–10 when Your mom told You to do something about the fact that there was no wine at the wedding, You obeyed her even though You said it wasn't the right time. It's hard for me to always honor and obey my parents as Ephesians 6:1–3 and the commandment in Exodus 20:12 say I should. But it's easier when I remember what You did.

Thank You for promising me a better and longer life if I honor my parents. John 19:26, 27 describe Your love for Your mother even as You were dying on the cross and asked John to take care of her. Lord, I want to love my folks like that, so please help me to respect and obey them. Thank You for hearing and answering my prayer. AMEN.

Promises About Dealing With Parents

*"My child, listen when your father corrects you. Don't neglect your
mother's instruction. What you learn from them will crown you
with grace and be a chain of honor around your neck"
(Proverbs 1:8, 9, NLT).*

*" 'But why did you need to search?' he asked. 'Didn't you know
that I must be in my Father's house?' But they didn't understand
what he meant" (Luke 2:49, 50, NLT).*

*" 'They have no more wine.'
'Dear woman, that's not our problem,' Jesus replied. 'My time has
not yet come' " (John 2:3, 4, NLT).*

*"Children, obey your parents in the Lord, for this is right.
'Honor your father and mother,' which is the first commandment
with promise: 'that it may be well with you and you may live
long on the earth' " (Ephesians 6:1–3, NKJV).*

*"He said to His mother, 'Woman, behold your son!' Then He said
to the disciple, 'Behold your mother!' And from that hour that
disciple took her to his own home" (John 19:26, 27, NKJV).*

Additional Scripture and Promises

Lev. 19:32	Prov. 13:1	Prov. 23:22
Lev. 20:9	Prov. 15:20	Eph. 6:1, 2
Prov. 4:1	Prov. 17:6	Matt. 15:4
Prov. 10:1	Prov. 19:13	Col. 3:20

DEATH

DEAR PRECIOUS SAVIOR,

I so desperately need to hear Your voice telling me everything will be OK. The doctors say I am dying and that only a miracle will save me. But God, You are a God of miracles, and I am asking that if it be Your will, please spare my life! I must confess, I don't want to die! But I know there are worse things than death. Being separated from You is worse than death, so Lord, I accept whatever plan You have for me.

Help me not to fear death because You have revealed to me in 1 Thessalonians 4:13 that I don't need to grieve for I will only be sleeping. In Revelation 14:13 there is a blessing on those who die in the Lord, for You will raise them from the grave so they can spend eternity with You. Oh Father, thank You for that blessed hope. You are my best Friend, and I trust You when You tell me in Isaiah 41:10 not to fear, for You are with me and that You will strengthen me.

I am claiming Your promise in 1 Corinthians 15:53, 54 that when the trumpet will sound, I will be changed and death will be swallowed up in victory! I can't wait to hear Your voice waking me up; I'm looking forward to meeting You face to face in the clouds of glory! Oh what a glorious day! Please wrap Your arms around me now, and let me feel the comfort of Your presence. AMEN.

Promises About Death

"But I do not want you to be ignorant, brethren, concerning those who have fallen asleep, lest you sorrow as others who have no hope" (1 Thessalonians 4:13, NKJV).

"Then I heard a voice from heaven saying to me, 'Write: "Blessed are the dead who die in the Lord from now on." ' 'Yes,' says the Spirit, 'that they may rest from their labors, and their works follow them' " (Revelation 14:13, NKJV).

" ' "Fear not, for I am with you; Be not dismayed, for I am your God. I will strengthen you, Yes, I will help you, I will uphold you with My righteous right hand" ' " (Isaiah 41:10, NKJV).

"In a flash, in the twinkling of an eye, at the last trumpet. For the trumpet will sound, the dead will be raised imperishable, and we will be changed. For the perishable must clothe itself with the imperishable, and the mortal with immortality. When the perishable has been clothed with the imperishable, and the mortal with immortality, then the saying that is written will come true: 'Death has been swallowed up in victory' "
(1 Corinthians 15:52–54, NIV).

Additional Scripture and Promises

Job 19:26, 27	*Isa. 35:10*	*John 16:20, 33*
Ps. 16:9, 10	*Isa. 49:13*	*Rom. 8:38, 39*
Ps. 17:15	*Isa. 51:11, 12*	*1 Cor. 15:52–57*
Ps. 23:4	*Isa. 61:1–3*	*2 Cor. 4:8, 16, 18*
Ps. 34:18	*Lam. 3:31–33*	*1 Thess. 4:13–16*
Ps. 48:14	*John 3:15*	*Heb. 4:15, 16*
Ps. 73:26	*John 5:28, 29*	*1 Pet. 5:7*
Isa. 25:8	*John 11:24, 25*	*Rev. 21:3, 4*

DEPRESSION

DEAR FATHER IN HEAVEN,

Everything in my life seems dreary, and I can't shake off this deep depression within me. Even though You have blessed me with much, I seem weighed down with a horrible feeling that everything around me is dark and that this world would be a better place without me in it! I can't seem to please anyone, much less myself! Nothing I do seems to be worth anything.

You have told me in Psalm 34:17 to cry out to You and that You will deliver me from all my troubles. Well Lord, I'm not just crying out, I'm screaming, "Please help me!" I'm claiming Your promise in Psalm 147:3 that You will heal my broken heart and bind up my wounds. Help me, Lord, to see that the glass is half full instead of half empty and to count my blessings, not my troubles. Let my heart believe You when You tell me in Isaiah 41:10 not to fear, because You are with me and You will strengthen me.

Oh precious Father, I need Your strength. I claim Your promise in Isaiah 51:11 that You will give me joy and that my sorrow and mourning will pass away! I am trusting You to take all my depressing thoughts away and to fill me with optimism and hope. And I'm thanking You in advance for what I know You are about to do! In Your holy name I pray. AMEN.

Promises About Depression

"The righteous cry out, and the LORD hears,
And delivers them out of all their troubles"
(Psalm 34:17, NKJV).

"He heals the brokenhearted and binds up their wounds"
(Psalm 147:3, NIV).

" ' "Fear not, for I am with you; Be not dismayed,
for I am your God. I will strengthen you, . . .
I will uphold you with My righteous right hand" ' "
(Isaiah 41:10, NKJV).

" 'The ransomed of the LORD will return.
They will enter Zion with singing;
everlasting joy will crown their heads.
Gladness and joy will overtake them,
and sorrow and sighing will flee away' "
(Isaiah 51:11, NIV).

Additional Scripture and Promises

Ps. 30:5, 8–12	*Rom. 8:38, 39*	*Heb. 13:5, 6*
Ps. 103:10, 12	*2 Cor. 1:3, 4*	*1 Pet. 4:12, 13*
Isa. 40:29–31	*2 Cor. 4:8, 9, 16–18*	*1 Pet. 5:6, 7*
Isa. 43:2	*Gal. 6:9*	*1 John 4:16*
Isa. 61:1–3	*Phil. 4:8, 12, 13*	
Matt. 11:28–30	*Heb. 6:15, 19*	

DISCERNMENT

DEAR PRECIOUS FATHER IN HEAVEN,

I am facing so many decisions, and I know that I have choices to make. But Lord, I don't know which way to go or what to do. When I look at all the information and listen to others, I am more confused than ever. I am pleading for understanding and discernment just as King Solomon did in 1 Kings 3:9, 28. Oh Father, bless me with the gift of discernment that I might know the difference between good and evil.

I know Satan would love to trick me into making decisions that would end up hurting me and others, so I am pleading for understanding and discernment to know Your will. John 16:13 says that the Spirit of truth will guide me into all truth. Oh Lord, I want Your Spirit of truth—Your Holy Spirit—to constantly direct my decision making.

My prayer to You, Oh Lord, is recorded in Philippians 1:9 and 10: "that [my] love may abound more and more in knowledge and depth of insight, so that [I] may be able to discern what is best and may be pure and blameless" (NIV). I do love You so very much, and I am trusting You for the answers that I need. In Your holy name I pray. AMEN.

Promises About Discernment

" 'Therefore give to Your servant an understanding heart to judge Your people, that I may discern between good and evil. For who is able to judge this great people of Yours?' . . . And all Israel heard of the judgment which the king had rendered; and they feared the king, for they saw that the wisdom of God was in him to administer justice" (1 Kings 3:9, 28, NKJV).

Jesus said, " 'But when he, the Spirit of truth, comes, he will guide you into all truth. He will not speak on his own; he will speak only what he hears, and he will tell you what is yet to come' " (John 16:13, NIV).

"This is my prayer: that your love may abound more and more in knowledge and depth of insight, so that you may be able to discern what is best and may be pure and blameless until the day of Christ" (Philippians 1:9, 10, NIV).

"There are diversities of gifts, but the same Spirit . . . to another the working of miracles, to another prophecy, to another discerning of spirits" (1 Corinthians 12:4, 10, NKJV).

Additional Scripture and Promises

1 Kings 3:7–28	Prov. 13:10, 15, 20	Dan. 12:3
Ps. 111:10	Prov. 16:21, 22	1 Cor. 2:11–16
Ps. 119:125	Prov. 18:15	1 Thess. 5:21, 22
Prov. 1:5	Prov. 19:8, 11	Phil. 1:9, 10
Prov. 2:11	Prov. 23:23	James 1:5
Prov. 3:21–24	Prov. 24:5	James 3:13, 17, 18
Prov. 9:10	Eccles. 7:11, 12	1 John 4:1, 2, 6
Prov. 10:13	Dan. 2:20, 21	1 John 5:20

DISCOURAGEMENT

DEAR PRECIOUS HEAVENLY FATHER,

You have given me so many wonderful blessings, and yet I cannot shake the discouragement that I feel right now. I know I should be strong and of good courage as You have told me to be in Joshua 1:9, because You are with me wherever I go. But Lord, today my heart is so heavy that I plead with You to lift me up as You have promised to do in Psalm 37:24 and to uphold me with Your hand.

In Lamentations 3:21–26 You have promised that Your mercies will keep me from destruction, so let me focus on the ray of hope provided by the assurance that Your compassion never ends because of the greatness of Your faithfulness! You have given me so much to look forward to, and I am claiming Your promise in John 14:1–3 that even now You are preparing a mansion in heaven for me to spend eternity there with You!

I am also claiming Philippians 4:13, which promises that I can do all things through You because You strengthen me! Thank You for giving me Your strength and power to face whatever lies before me. In Your name I pray. AMEN.

Promises About Discouragement

" 'Have I not commanded you? Be strong and of good courage; do not be afraid, nor be dismayed, for the LORD your God is with you wherever you go' " (Joshua 1:9, NKJV).

"Though he fall, he shall not be utterly cast down; For the LORD upholds him with His hand" (Psalm 37:24, NKJV).

"Yet there is one ray of hope: his compassion never ends. It is only the Lord's mercies that have kept us from complete destruction. Great is his faithfulness; his lovingkindness begins afresh each day. My soul claims the Lord as my inheritance; therefore I will hope in him. The Lord is wonderfully good to those who wait for him, to those who seek for him. It is good both to hope and wait quietly for the salvation of the Lord" (Lamentations 3:21–26, TLB).

" 'Let not your heart be troubled; you believe in God, believe also in Me. In My Father's house are many mansions; if it were not so, I would have told you. I go to prepare a place for you. And if I go and prepare a place for you, I will come again and receive you to Myself; that where I am, there you may be also' " (John 14:1–3, NKJV).

Additional Scripture and Promises

Exod. 33:14	Ps. 121	Matt. 10:29–31
Deut. 20:4	Ps. 124:2–8	John 14:27
Job 5:19–22	Ps. 145:14	Rom. 8:15
Ps. 1:1–3	Prov. 3:25, 26	Rom. 15:4
Ps. 18:33–36	Isa. 40:29–31	2 Cor. 4:6–10
Ps. 27:1	Isa. 41:10, 13	Phil. 4:12, 13
Ps. 46:1, 2	Isa. 42:16	2 Tim. 1:7
Ps. 46:10	Jer. 29:11	
Ps. 56:3, 4	Jer. 33:3	

DIVORCE

DEAR FATHER IN HEAVEN,

I stare blankly at these divorce papers, and I'm numb with pain. I can't hide my brokenness from You, for I am deeply hurt with the sting of rejection. Loneliness consumes me. I felt that even You had forsaken me until I read Your affirming promise in Hebrews 13:5 that You will never leave me nor forsake me. Just knowing that You won't leave me is so comforting.

I found another promise in Jeremiah 31:3, 4 in which You say, " 'Yes, I have loved you with an everlasting love; . . . I will build you, and you shall be rebuilt' " (NKJV). I hold on to that promise even though my eyes are so blurred with tears I can't imagine happiness again, much less being rebuilt! I don't want this divorce, and You have made it very clear how You feel about divorce in Malachi 2:16: " 'For the LORD God of Israel says That He hates divorce' " (NKJV). Lord, please forgive me for whatever I have done that has led to this life-changing decision.

If there is anything that I can do to save my marriage, please reveal it to me. I want, at least, to try! But if divorce happens, please give me the strength and courage to accept it, knowing that You will be with me every step of the way. Heal my heart, precious Jesus, that I may be whole again and filled with Your gift of joy that You want me to have. I lay hold of Your precious promise in Hosea 2:19, 20 that You will betroth me to You forever. I am trusting You to get me through—one day at a time! AMEN.

Promises About Divorce

"For He Himself has said, 'I will never leave you nor forsake you' "
(Hebrews 13:5, NKJV).

" 'Yes, I have loved you with an everlasting love; Therefore with lovingkindness I have drawn you. Again I will build you, and you shall be rebuilt' " (Jeremiah 31:3, 4, NKJV).

" 'For the LORD God of Israel says That He hates divorce' "
(Malachi 2:16, NKJV).

" 'I will betroth you to me forever;
I will betroth you in righteousness and justice,
in love and compassion.
I will betroth you in faithfulness,
and you will acknowledge the LORD' "
(Hosea 2:19, 20, NIV).

Additional Scripture and Promises

Gen. 1:27, 28   *Jer. 3:1*   *Rom. 7:2, 3*
Gen. 2:18, 21–25   *Mal. 2:14–16*   *1 Cor. 7:2, 10–17, 39*
Num. 14:18   *Matt. 5:31, 32*   *Col. 3:13*
Deut. 24:1–4   *Matt. 19:3–9*   *Heb. 13:4*
2 Chron. 7:14   *Mark 10:2–12*   *1 Pet. 3:7*
Eccles. 4:9   *Luke 16:18*

DOUBT

DEAR HEAVENLY FATHER,

I find it difficult to come to You in prayer because I'm not really sure I believe that You will help me. I know that You are God and can do anything, but in my heart I sometimes question whether what I want is Your will or whether I'm important enough for You to work a miracle in my behalf. I know You say in Matthew 21:22 that whatever I ask in prayer, believing, I will receive! It is the "believing" that I struggle with.

Lord, my prayer is Jude 22: "Be merciful to those who doubt" (NIV). Please be merciful to me! I feel like the father in Mark 9:24 who cried out, " 'Lord, I believe; help my unbelief!' " (NKJV). You had mercy on that father and honored his tiny bit of faith by healing his son. Thank You, Lord, for not withholding a miracle because his faith wasn't perfect. It gives me hope that You will honor my requests as my faith grows. I want to have a strong faith. I want to believe Your words in Mark 5:36 in which You plead with me " 'not to be afraid; only believe' " (NKJV).

Help me to put away all my fears and doubts. Give me the strength and courage to believe and trust in You. I want to have the same kind of faith and belief that You talk about in Mark 11:23—the faith that can say to a mountain, " ' "Go, throw yourself into the sea" ' " (NIV), and it would happen! Precious Father, I am reaching out to You, knowing and trusting that You alone can erase all doubt from my heart. AMEN.

Promises About Doubt

"And all things, whatsoever ye shall ask in prayer, believing, ye shall receive" (Matthew 21:22, KJV).

"Be merciful to those who doubt" (Jude 22, NIV).

"Jesus said to him, 'If you can believe, all things are possible to him who believes.' Immediately the father of the child cried out and said with tears, 'Lord, I believe; help my unbelief!' " (Mark 9:23, 24, NKJV).

"Jesus told the synagogue ruler, 'Don't be afraid; just believe' " (Mark 5:36, NIV).

"Jesus answered. 'I tell you the truth, if anyone says to this mountain, "Go, throw yourself into the sea," and does not doubt in his heart but believes that what he says will happen, it will be done for him' " (Mark 11:22, 23, NIV).

Additional Scripture and Promises

Ps. 18:30	Matt. 28:20	1 Thess. 5:24
Prov. 3:26	Luke 12:6, 7, 29–31	Heb. 3:12
Isa. 30:15	Luke 17:5, 6	Heb. 10:23
Isa. 55:10, 11	John 7:17	1 Pet. 4:12, 13
Isa. 59:1	Rom. 3:3, 4	2 Pet. 3:9, 16
Matt. 14:31	Rom. 4:20, 21	
Matt. 21:21	Rom. 10:17	

FAITH

DEAR GOD IN HEAVEN,

It's so easy to have faith in You when everything is going my way. I love You, Lord, I really do. So, I don't understand why I have so much trouble trusting You when I'm experiencing trials in my life. I want to have the kind of faith that You speak of in Matthew 17:20—faith as small as a tiny mustard seed, but that can move mountains!

When You work an obvious miracle in my life, it is easy for me to praise You and have faith that You have intervened on my behalf. But I now realize that is not really faith. Your description of faith in Hebrews 11:1 is so very clear: "Faith is being sure of what we hope for and certain of what we do not see" (NIV). Please help me to trust You more, especially during the times in my life that are so dark that I cannot see You working. Help me to reach out and hold Your hand, knowing with absolute certainty that You will guide me on the right path.

Most of all, when my faith is weak, remind me, Lord, of Your precious promise in Ephesians 2:8, 9 that it is by grace that I have been saved, through faith which is the gift of God. Oh precious Jesus, I want my faith in You to be so strong that I may receive Your gift of salvation. Thank You for never giving up on me—and thank You most of all for Your love, grace, and mercy. AMEN.

Promises About Faith

"He replied, 'Because you have so little faith. I tell you the truth, if you have faith as small as a mustard seed, you can say to this mountain, "Move from here to there" and it will move. Nothing will be impossible for you'" (Matthew 17:20, NIV).

"Now faith is the substance of things hoped for, the evidence of things not seen" (Hebrews 11:1, NKJV).

"For it is by grace you have been saved, through faith— and this not from yourselves, it is the gift of God—not by works, so that no one can boast" (Ephesians 2:8, 9, NIV).

Additional Scripture and Promises

Matt. 15:28	*1 Cor. 2:5*	*1 Thess. 5:8*
Matt. 17:17–20	*1 Cor. 16:13*	*1 Tim. 6:12*
Mark 11:22–24	*2 Cor. 1:24*	*2 Tim. 4:7, 8*
Luke 7:9, 50	*2 Cor. 5:7*	*Heb. 11*
John 14:12	*Gal. 2:20*	*James 1:3–8*
Rom. 1:17	*Eph. 2:8, 9*	*James 2:17–22*
Rom. 3:22	*Eph. 6:16*	*James 5:14, 15*
Rom. 5:1, 2	*Col. 2:5–7*	*Rev. 2:19*

FAITHFULNESS

PRECIOUS HEAVENLY FATHER,

Even though You rule the universe, You always make time for me. You know my innermost thoughts and desires, and it amazes me that You want to be a part of every detail of my life. When I mess up, You are there to forgive me and help me to do what is right. Every morning You give me a brand-new robe of Your righteousness to wear. Great is Your faithfulness!

Oh, Lord, my song is Psalm 89:1: "With my mouth will I make known Your faithfulness to all generations" (NKJV). Please keep me true to You. I claim the promise in Proverbs 2:8 that You will continue to guard my course and keep me faithful to You. I know that on my own I will fail You. So please fulfill Your promise to me in Proverbs 3:3 and 4 to bind Your love and faithfulness around my neck so that they will never leave me, so that I will have favor and a good name in Your sight and in the sight of others.

I want to be like You, Lord. I want to be faithful in what I do and follow through on what I say, so someday I can hear You speak to me the words recorded in Matthew 25:23: " ' "Well done, good and faithful servant; . . . Enter into the joy of your lord" ' " (NKJV). I ask for all these blessings in Jesus' name. AMEN.

PROMISES ABOUT FAITHFULNESS

*"I will sing of the mercies of the LORD forever; With my mouth will
I make known Your faithfulness to all generations"
(Psalm 89:1, NKJV).*

*"[God] guards the course of the just and protects the way of his
faithful ones" (Proverbs 2:8, NIV).*

*"Let love and faithfulness never leave you; bind them around
your neck, write them on the tablet of your heart. Then you will
win favor and a good name in the sight of God and man"
(Proverbs 3:3, 4, NIV).*

*" 'His lord said to him, "Well done, good and faithful servant; you
have been faithful over a few things, I will make you ruler over many
things. Enter into the joy of your lord" ' " (Matthew 25:23, NKJV).*

ADDITIONAL SCRIPTURE AND PROMISES

1 Sam. 26:23	*Prov. 3:3, 4*	*1 Thess. 5:24*
2 Sam. 22:26	*Prov. 14:22*	*2 Thess. 3:3*
Ps. 31:23	*Prov. 28:20*	*2 Tim. 2:13*
Ps. 36:5	*Isa. 25:1*	*Heb. 10:23*
Ps. 86:15	*Lam. 3:22, 23*	*1 John 1:9*
Ps. 89:1, 2	*Matt. 25:21*	*Rev. 2:10*
Ps. 91:4	*1 Cor. 10:13*	*Rev. 13:10*
Ps. 145:13	*Gal. 5:22, 23*	*Rev. 17:14*

FAMILY

Dear Father in Heaven,

Thank You for letting me be part of Your family, for lavishing Your love upon me and calling me Your child in 1 John 3:1. It makes me feel so special. Romans 8:15, 16 reminds me that You could have made me a slave so that I'd serve You with fear—for You are an awesome, powerful, and mighty God. But instead, You made me Your child, so I can love and trust You as children love and trust their parents.

At anytime I can call to You, "Abba, Father," and You will take care of me. Oh Father, hold me in Your loving arms, and may I always feel warm and secure knowing I belong to You. And may my children feel the same about me!

Thank You for each member of my family. Give me the dedication and commitment to You to say as Joshua did in Joshua 24:15, " 'As for me and my house, we will serve the LORD' " (NKJV). Help me to keep Your law in my heart and to continually remind my family of Your commandments as Deuteronomy 6:6–9 tells me to do, so that our family will never forget the rules that will help us live together happily.

Finally, I claim for my family the promise in Deuteronomy 4:40 that if we obey Your law, all will go well for us and we'll enjoy life together on this earth—and for eternity with You in heaven. AMEN.

Promises About Family

"How great is the love the Father has lavished on us, that we should be called children of God! And that is what we are!" (1 John 3:1, NIV).

"You did not receive a spirit that makes you a slave again to fear, but you received the Spirit of sonship. And by him we cry, 'Abba, Father.' The Spirit himself testifies with our spirit that we are God's children" (Romans 8:15, 16, NIV).

" 'Choose for yourselves this day whom you will serve, . . . But as for me and my house, we will serve the LORD' " (Joshua 24:15, NKJV).

" 'You shall therefore keep His statutes and His commandments which I command you today, that it may go well with you and with your children after you, and that you may prolong your days in the land which the LORD your God is giving you for all time' " (Deuteronomy 4:40, NKJV).

" 'And these words which I command you today shall be in your heart. You shall teach them diligently to your children' " (Deuteronomy 6:6, 7, NKJV).

Additional Scripture and Promises

Gen. 18:19	Prov. 10:1	Matt. 10:37
Exod. 20:12	Prov. 13:22	Eph. 5:21–6:4
Deut. 6:6–9	Prov. 17:6	Gal. 6:10
Ps. 27:10	Prov. 20:7	1 Tim. 3:4, 5
Ps. 103:13	Prov. 22:6	1 Tim. 5:8
Ps. 127	Prov. 23:22, 24	Heb. 2:11
Ps. 128	Prov. 29:17	1 John 2:10
Prov. 3:11, 12	Isa. 54:13	
Prov. 4:1	Mal. 4:6	

FEAR

DEAR LORD, MY GOD,

I come to You because I need You to take away this terrible fear that I can't seem to overcome. I need You to replace this fear with Your peace and confidence. I understand Your Word says in Psalm 27:1 that You are my Light and my Salvation—so I shouldn't be afraid. But You know what's happening to me right now and that I'm really scared.

That's why I'm claiming Your promise in Isaiah 41:10 that I have no reason to fear because You are with me. Thank You for always being there for me—and for sending Your angels to surround me as Psalm 34:7 promises. In Psalm 46:1 You have promised to be my Refuge and my Strength and to help me when I'm in trouble.

Lord, let me feel You holding me up with Your righteous right hand. I love Your promise in Isaiah 35:3, 4 that when my hands and knees are shaking in fear, You will come and save me, bringing vengeance and divine retribution against my foes. Thank You for that assurance. I love You, precious heavenly Father. AMEN.

Promises About Fear

"The LORD is my light and my salvation;
Whom shall I fear? The LORD is the strength of my life;
Of whom shall I be afraid?" (Psalm 27:1, NKJV).

" ' "Fear not, for I am with you; Be not dismayed, for I am your
God. I will strengthen you, Yes, I will help you, I will uphold you
with My righteous right hand" ' " (Isaiah 41:10, NKJV).

"The angel of the LORD encamps all around those who fear Him,
And delivers them" (Psalm 34:7, NKJV).

"God is our refuge and strength, A very present help in trouble.
Therefore we will not fear, Even though the earth be removed,
And though the mountains be carried into the midst of the sea"
(Psalm 46:1, 2, NKJV).

"Strengthen the feeble hands, steady the knees that give way; say
to those with fearful hearts, 'Be strong, do not fear; your God
will come, he will come with vengeance; with divine retribution
he will come to save you' " (Isaiah 35:3, 4, NIV).

Additional Scripture and Promises

Gen. 28:15	*Ps. 112:7*	*Matt. 11:28*
Deut. 31:6–8	*Ps. 121:7, 8*	*Mark 4:40*
2 Kings 6:15–17	*Prov. 1:33*	*Rom. 8:31, 32*
Job 11:13–20	*Prov. 3:24*	*Phil. 4:13*
Ps. 3:3, 5, 6	*Prov. 18:10*	*2 Tim. 1:7*
Ps. 4:8	*Isa. 41:11, 13*	*Heb. 13:6*
Ps. 32:7	*Isa. 43:2*	*1 Pet. 3:13, 14*
Ps. 56:3	*Matt. 10:29–31*	*Jude 24*

FINANCES

DEAR LORD,

I have tried to manage my finances wisely, but I'm facing some challenges—and I just don't see how I'm going to make it. So I'm claiming Your promise in Psalm 34:9, 10 that those who seek You will not lack any good thing. I'm also claiming the words of Matthew 6:8 that You know the things I need before I even ask, and the promise of Philippians 4:19 that You will meet all my needs "according to [the] glorious riches in Christ Jesus" (NIV).

You've said there is no need for me to worry, so I'm holding on to Your words in Matthew 6:32–34 that if I seek first Your kingdom and Your righteousness, You'll give me everything else I need.

My prayer is Habakkuk's prayer: "I am filled with awe by your amazing works. In this time of our deep need, help us again as you did in years gone by" (Habakkuk 3:2, NLT). Show us Your power. I praise You for the miracles You are in the process of working for me, as I hold on to Your promise in Habakkuk 2:3 that I should wait patiently for "it will surely take place. It will not be delayed" (NLT). Thank You, God, for that assurance. AMEN.

Promises About Finances

"Oh, fear the Lord, *you His saints! There is no want to those who fear Him. The young lions lack and suffer hunger; But those who seek the* Lord *shall not lack any good thing"* (Psalm 34:9, 10, NKJV).

" 'For your Father knows the things you have need of before you ask Him' " (Matthew 6:8, NKJV).

"My God will meet all your needs according to his glorious riches in Christ Jesus" (Philippians 4:19, NIV).

" 'Therefore I say to you, do not worry about your life, what you will eat or what you will drink; nor about your body, what you will put on. . . . . But seek first the kingdom of God and His righteousness, and all these things shall be added to you. Therefore do not worry about tomorrow, for tomorrow will worry about its own things. Sufficient for the day is its own trouble' " (Matthew 6:25–34, NKJV).

"I am filled with awe by your amazing works. In this time of our deep need, help us again as you did in years gone by. And in your anger, remember your mercy" (Habakkuk 3:2, NLT).

Additional Scripture and Promises

FORGIVENESS

PRECIOUS LORD,

Only You can take the anger out of my heart and give me forgiveness. I feel defensive and revengeful when people say or do things that hurt me. There is no desire in me to forgive them, especially when it happens again and again. It seems impossible to follow Your admonition in Matthew 18:21 and 22 that I should forgive "seventy times seven."

And then I remember what people did to You. Your enemies spit on You, cursed You, and even lied about You! Yet You said in Luke 23:34, " 'Father, forgive them, for they do not know what they are doing' "(NIV). I am longing to be like You. Remove this hardness in my heart. You are the only One who can help me. I lay hold of the promise of 1 John 1:9 that if I confess my sins, You are faithful and just and will forgive me from my sins and purify me from all my unrighteousness.

I confess my unforgiving heart and claim the promise in Matthew 6:14 that if I forgive others when they sin against me, then You will also forgive me. Thank You for melting the anger inside me and creating in me a pure heart as David prayed in Psalm 51:10–12. You are such an awesome God, and I am grateful for Your forgiveness that You put in my heart for others. With all my heart, I thank You. AMEN.

Promises About Forgiveness

"Then came Peter to him, and said, Lord, how oft shall my brother sin against me, and I forgive him? till seven times? Jesus saith . . . Until seventy times seven" (Matthew 18:21, 22, KJV).

"If we confess our sins, [God] is faithful and just and will forgive us our sins and purify us from all unrighteousness" (1 John 1:9, NIV).

" 'If you forgive men when they sin against you, your heavenly Father will also forgive you' " (Matthew 6:14, NIV).

"Create in me a pure heart, O God, and renew a steadfast spirit within me. Do not cast me from your presence or take your Holy Spirit from me. Restore to me the joy of your salvation and grant me a willing spirit, to sustain me" (Psalm 51:10–12, NIV).

Additional Scripture and Promises

Num. 14:18	Micah 7:18, 19	Luke 23:34
Ps. 32:1, 2, 5	Matt. 5:7, 39	Acts 3:19
Ps. 86:5	Matt. 5:44, 45	Acts 10:43
Isa. 1:18	Matt. 6:12–15	2 Cor. 2:7
Isa. 43:25	Matt. 12:31, 32	Eph. 4:32
Isa. 55:7	Mark 11:25	Col. 3:13
Jer. 31:34	Luke 7:42, 47	Heb. 8:12
Dan. 9:9	Luke 17:3, 4	James 5:16

FORSAKEN

Dear Almighty God,

It seems as if I don't have any friends and everyone has turned against me. I feel so empty inside. Lord, I have no strength to face this battle alone, so I'm claiming Your promise in Deuteronomy 31:6 in which You say that I don't have to be afraid of those who are against me because You will give me strength. And I claim the words of Psalm 9:10 that you will never forsake anyone who seeks You—and Lord, I am seeking You right now.

I'm holding on to Your promise in 2 Corinthians 4:9 that even though I'm in a tough situation, I will survive. Give me the courage of the apostle Paul to say and believe what he said: "We are hard-pressed on every side, yet not crushed; we are perplexed, but not in despair; persecuted, but not forsaken; struck down, but not destroyed" (2 Corinthians 4:8, 9, NKJV).

Thank You, Lord, for the reassurance of Your abundant love in Isaiah 41:17, 18—that You hear me and won't forsake me. You love me so much that even when I am thirsty in a dry land, You will not just give me a drink, but You'll open rivers, fountains, and springs of water! Thank You for filling me with Your love. Amen.

PROMISES ABOUT BEING FORSAKEN

" 'Be strong and of good courage, do not fear nor be afraid of
them; for the LORD your God, He is the One who goes with you.
He will not leave you or forsake you' "
(Deuteronomy 31:6, NKJV).

"Those who know your name will trust in you, for you, LORD,
have never forsaken those who seek you" (Psalm 9:10, NIV).

"We are hard-pressed on every side, yet not crushed; we are
perplexed, but not in despair; persecuted, but not forsaken;
struck down, but not destroyed" (2 Corinthians 4:8, 9, NKJV).

" 'The poor and needy seek water, but there is none,
Their tongues fail for thirst.
I, the LORD, will hear them;
I, the God of Israel, will not forsake them.
I will open rivers in desolate heights,
And fountains in the midst of the valleys;
I will make the wilderness a pool of water,
And the dry land springs of water' "
(Isaiah 41:17, 18, NKJV).

ADDITIONAL SCRIPTURE AND PROMISES

Deut. 4:31	Ps. 94:14	Luke 10:16
1 Sam. 12:22	Isa. 49:15, 16	John 3:16
Ps. 4:3	Isa. 53:3	John 6:37–39
Ps. 13:3–6	Jer. 31:3	Rom. 8:38, 39
Ps. 27:9, 10	Hosea 11:4	Eph. 3:17–19
Ps. 37:25	Zeph. 3:17	Heb. 13:5, 6
Ps. 43:5	Matt. 28:20	1 Pet. 5:7
Ps. 91:14, 15	Luke 6:20, 22	1 John 3:16–18

FRIENDSHIP

DEAR LOVING FATHER,

I long to have friends in my life who will strengthen me spiritually. It's so hard to find friends who are loyal and trustworthy. The sting of betrayal is so painful that sometimes my wall is too high for me to trust. Please teach me how to be a good friend. Proverbs 18:24 says that to have friends, I must be friendly. And Proverbs 13:20 warns me that I should choose my friends carefully because "He who walks with the wise grows wise; but a companion of fools suffers harm" (NIV). Please give me wisdom to discern a good friend from a fool!

Lord, it is my desire to be the kind of friend that my friends need! I want to have the loyalty of Jonathan, who loved David as much as his own soul and who was willing to give up his throne and life for his friend (1 Samuel 20:17–42).

Help me to pass the three tests of a true friend given in Your Word: " 'Greater love has no one than this, that he lay down his life for his friends' " (John 15:13, NIV). "A friend loves at all times" (Proverbs 17:17, NIV). And "Honor one another above yourselves" (Romans 12:10, NIV).

Oh Father, help me to choose friends that will draw me closer to You and let me be the kind of friend who always reflects Your character. In Your precious name I pray. AMEN.

PROMISES ABOUT FRIENDSHIP

"A man who has friends must himself be friendly,
But there is a friend who sticks closer than a brother"
(Proverbs 18:24, NKJV).

"He who walks with the wise grows wise, but a companion
of fools suffers harm" (Proverbs 13:20, NIV).

" 'Greater love has no one than this, that he
lay down his life for his friends' " (John 15:13, NIV).

"A friend loves at all times"
(Proverbs 17:17, NIV).

"Be devoted to one another in brotherly love.
Honor one another above yourselves"
(Romans 12:10, NIV).

ADDITIONAL SCRIPTURE AND PROMISES

Job 6:14	Luke 21:16	Col. 2:2, 3
Ps. 1:1	Rom. 13:8–10	1 Thess. 2:8
Ps. 118:8	Rom. 15:5–7	James 2:23
Ps. 133:1	1 Cor. 16:14	James 4:4
Prov. 16:28	2 Cor. 6:14	1 Pet. 3:8
Prov. 22:11, 24, 25	Eph. 3:14–19	1 Pet. 4:8
Eccles. 4:9–12	Eph. 4:1–4	1 John 1:5–7
Micah 7:5, 6	Phil. 2:1, 2	1 John 3:11, 16–18

FRIENDSHIP
WITH JESUS

MY PRECIOUS JESUS,

Oh how much I look forward to our special time together
each day when I take time to read Your Word and we talk
together. My favorite message about You is John 3:16. I like
to make it personal, by reading it like this: "For God so loved
me that He gave His only begotten Son, Jesus, that whoever
believes in Him should not perish, but have everlasting life."

Lord, do You know how special that makes me feel? My
heart is overwhelmed with gratitude. Imagine! The Creator
and God of the universe is always there for me supplying my
every need—just as You have promised in Philippians 4:19.
You are interested in whatever I'm doing, ever cheering me
on to my heavenly home.

My lips give praise to You as David did in Psalm 63:3,
"Because Your lovingkindness is better than life" (NKJV).
You have taught me what real love is because You are my
best Friend! Your Word in John 15:13–15 speaks to the
deepest part of my soul. You have said, " 'Greater love has
no one than this, than to lay down one's life for his friends' "
(NKJV). And Lord, You did that for me!

My heart rejoices and overflows with love for You. Even
though my earthly friends may disappoint me, I know You
never will! I love You, my Savior and dearest Friend! AMEN.

Promises About Friendship With Jesus

" 'For God so loved the world that He gave His only begotten
Son, that whoever believes in Him should not perish but have
everlasting life' " (John 3:16, NKJV).

"And my God shall supply all your need according to
His riches in glory by Christ Jesus" (Philippians 4:19, NKJV).

"Because Your lovingkindness is better than life,
My lips shall praise You" (Psalm 63:3, NKJV).

" 'Greater love has no one than this, than to lay down one's life
for his friends. You are My friends if you do whatever I
command you. No longer do I call you servants, for a servant
does not know what his master is doing;
but I have called you friends, for all things that I heard from
My Father I have made known to you' "
(John 15:13–15, NKJV).

Additional Scripture and Promises

Prov. 13:20	Mark 3:13–19, 33–35	John 2:1–9
Prov. 17:17	Mark 6:53–56	John 4:7–14
Prov. 18:24	Mark 14:32–42	John 6:15–21
Prov. 22:11	Luke 5:1–11, 27–32	John 10:14, 15
Matt. 8:23–27	Luke 8:1–3, 19–21	John 11:38–44
Matt. 9:10	Luke 19:1–10	John 14:19–24
Matt. 12:49, 50	Luke 24:13–43	John 17
Matt. 18:20	John 1:14	Rom. 12:10

THE FUTURE

Our Father Who Art in Heaven,

Oh, how much I want to be in heaven with You! Thank You, Lord, for Your promise in Jeremiah 29:11: " 'For I know the plans I have for you. . . . They are plans for good and not for disaster, to give you a future and a hope' " (NLT). That gives me courage, because even though I don't know what the future holds, I know who holds the future! But Lord, my hope is not for this world. I've already transferred my citizenship to heaven, as Philippians 3:20 says!

I'm homesick for heaven, and I pray that Your coming will be soon. I've had enough of sickness and sorrow, aches and pains, death and divorce, wars and crime, and all the violence and other evil things which just keep getting worse! Oh, how I long for heaven!

I can't even imagine what it's going to be like to have no more death, mourning, crying, or pain as Revelation 21:4 says! When I read 1 Corinthians 2:9 and 10, I can hardly wait! " 'No eye has seen, no ear has heard, no mind has conceived what God has prepared for those who love him' " (NIV). And 1 John 3:2 says, "We are children of God, and what we will be has not yet been made known. But we know that when he appears, we shall be like him" (NIV).

What wonderful promises! Oh Lord, come quickly. I love You and want to live with You forever. What an incredible future to look forward to! Amen.

Promises About the Future

" 'For I know the plans I have for you,' says the Lord. 'They are plans for good and not for disaster, to give you a future and a hope' " (Jeremiah 29:11, NLT).

"Our citizenship is in heaven. And we eagerly await a Savior from there, the Lord Jesus Christ, who, by the power that enables him to bring everything under his control, will transform our lowly bodies so that they will be like his glorious body" (Philippians 3:20, 21, NIV).

"There will be no more death or mourning or crying or pain, for the old order of things has passed away" (Revelation 21:4, NIV).

"As it is written: 'No eye has seen, no ear has heard, no mind has conceived what God has prepared for those who love him'—but God has revealed it to us by his Spirit. The Spirit searches all things, even the deep things of God" (1 Corinthians 2:9, 10, NIV).

"We are children of God, and what we will be has not yet been made known. But we know that when he appears, we shall be like him, for we shall see him as he is" (1 John 3:2, NIV).

Additional Scripture and Promises

Job 19:25, 26	Dan. 2:44	2 Cor. 5:17
Ps. 139:16	Dan. 7:13, 14	1 Thess. 4:16, 17
Isa. 25:9	Zeph. 1:14	Titus 2:13, 14
Isa. 29:18	Mal. 4:5	James 4:14, 15
Isa. 30:18	Matt. 16:27	1 Pet. 5:4
Isa. 40:5, 10	Acts 1:11	1 John 3:2
Isa. 59:21	1 Cor. 3:21–23	Rev. 1:7
Isa. 66:22	1 Cor. 15:51, 52	Rev. 22:7–12

GENEROSITY

DEAR HEAVENLY FATHER,

You have blessed me with so many blessings. I may not be wealthy in financial terms, but You have certainly supplied all my needs just as You have promised. Lord, I want to be used by You. Please plant a generous spirit within my heart and remove all selfishness within me. In 2 Corinthians 9:11, it's clear that You have made me "rich" in every way for one major purpose—so I can be generous with others and praise You with thanksgiving.

I find in Acts 20:35 and 2 Corinthians 9:6 the principles by which I want to live my life: " ' "It is more blessed to give than to receive" ' " (NIV), and "whoever sows generously will also reap generously" (NIV).

Your promise in Proverbs 11:25 is that a generous person will prosper. You add to this the promise in Luke 6:38, " 'Give, and it will be given to you' " (NIV). As I claim these promises, I realize that You can use me to spread Your blessings. What an honor this is! Lord, bring into my life the people You desire to bless.

When You tell me to give, help me to be generous. Don't let my perception of whether a person has real needs get in the way of passing on the blessings that You have planned should flow through me. Thank You for using me in this incredible way. AMEN.

Promises About Generosity

"You will be made rich in every way so that you can be generous on every occasion, and through us your generosity will result in thanksgiving to God" (2 Corinthians 9:11, NIV).

"It is more blessed to give than to receive" (Acts 20:35, KJV).

"Whoever sows sparingly will also reap sparingly, and whoever sows generously will also reap generously" (2 Corinthians 9:6, NIV).

"A generous man will prosper; he who refreshes others will himself be refreshed" (Proverbs 11:25, NIV).

" 'Give, and it will be given to you: good measure, pressed down, shaken together, and running over will be put into your bosom. For with the same measure that you use, it will be measured back to you' " (Luke 6:38, NKJV).

Additional Scripture and Promises

Exod. 35:29	*Prov. 14:21*	*Mark 10:21*
Deut. 14:29	*Prov. 19:17*	*Luke 6:30*
Deut. 16:10	*Prov. 22:9*	*Luke 12:33*
Ps. 37: 21, 25, 26	*Prov. 28:27*	*Luke 14:13, 14*
Ps. 41:1, 2	*Eccles. 11:1*	*Rom. 12:6, 8*
Ps. 112:5, 9	*Isa. 58:7, 8, 10*	*2 Cor. 9:7*
Ps. 116:12–14	*Matt. 6:1–4*	*1 Tim. 6:17–19*
Prov. 11:24, 25	*Matt. 25:34–40*	

GENTLENESS

Dear Loving Savior,

Being gentle doesn't come naturally to me. Sometimes I rush into situations and tend to push my own agenda. Forgive me, Lord. Help me to be more like the Shepherd described in Isaiah 40:11 when I'm dealing with others—especially those who have fragile spirits. Isaiah says "He [God] tends his flock like a shepherd: He gathers the lambs in his arms and carries them close to his heart; he gently leads those that have young" (NIV).

I pray that Your Holy Spirit will help me treat people in the gentle manner of this Shepherd. Give me discernment regarding the feelings of others and how to be gentle with them, rather than harsh and overbearing. Lord, You are all powerful; You created everything; You control the universe, and yet in Matthew 11:29 You describe Yourself as gentle and humble in heart and invite us to learn from You and to put on Your yoke, which will make it easier for us to pull our loads. In Colossians 3:12, You make it clear that Your chosen people will be gentle. And you say in 1 Peter 3:4 that a gentle and quiet spirit has unfading beauty.

Even though gentleness does not come naturally to me, my prayer is that as I draw closer to You, and as You live within me, that Your gentleness, through me, will be evident to all, as Philippians 4:5 says. Thank You for hearing and answering my prayer. In Jesus' name I pray. Amen.

Promises About Gentleness

"He tends his flock like a shepherd: He gathers the lambs in his arms and carries them close to his heart; he gently leads those that have young" (Isaiah 40:11, NIV).

Jesus said, " 'Take my yoke upon you and learn from me, for I am gentle and humble in heart, and you will find rest for your souls' " (Matthew 11:29, NIV).

"As God's chosen people, holy and dearly loved, clothe yourselves with compassion, kindness, humility, gentleness and patience" (Colossians 3:12, NIV).

"[Your beauty] should be that of your inner self, the unfading beauty of a gentle and quiet spirit, which is of great worth in God's sight" (1 Peter 3:4, NIV).

"Let your gentleness be evident to all. The Lord is near" (Philippians 4:5, NIV).

Additional Scripture and Promises

2 Sam. 18:5	2 Cor. 10:1	2 Tim. 2:24
2 Sam. 22:36	Gal. 5:22, 23	Titus 3:2
Ps. 18:35	Eph. 4:2	James 3:7
Ps. 37:11	1 Thess. 2:7	1 Pet. 1:18
Prov. 15:1	1 Tim. 6:11, 12	1 Pet. 3:15, 16

GOD'S LOVE

DEAR LOVING HEAVENLY FATHER,

You are holy and gracious and compassionate—and I hear You saying to me the words of a bridegroom in Hosea 2:19: " 'I will betroth you to me forever; I will betroth you in righteousness and justice, in love and compassion' " (NIV). Thank You, precious Lord, for lavishing on me such extravagant love. I want to be Yours forever. And when I read Zephaniah 3:17, I find myself falling in love with You even more: " 'The LORD your God is with you, he is mighty to save. He will take great delight in you, he will quiet you with his love, he will rejoice over you with singing' " (NIV). How can I not respond to such a compassionate God?

Thank You for being crazy about me, for seeing so much potential in me, and adorning me as Your bride with Your pure white robe of righteousness. Even though I make mistakes, You say in Micah 7:19 that You'll still love me and "will again have compassion on [me]" (NIV). In fact, You "will tread [my] sins underfoot and hurl all [my] iniquities into the depths of the sea" (NIV). How blessed I am to be loved so much that You're willing to forgive and forget my past sins.

I claim Your promise in Isaiah 54:10: " 'Though the mountains be shaken and the hills be removed, yet my unfailing love for you will not be shaken nor my covenant of peace be removed' " (NIV). Thank You, my precious Savior, for Your compassionate love. AMEN.

Promises About God's Love

" *'I will betroth you to me forever; I will betroth you in righteousness and justice, in love and compassion'* "
(Hosea 2:19, NIV).

" *'The L<small>ORD</small> your God is with you, he is mighty to save. He will take great delight in you, he will quiet you with his love; he will rejoice over you with singing'* "
(Zephaniah 3:17, NIV).

"You will again have compassion on us; you will tread our sins underfoot and hurl all our iniquities into the depths of the sea"
(Micah 7:19, NIV).

" *'Though the mountains be shaken and the hills be removed, yet my unfailing love for you will not be shaken nor my covenant of peace be removed,' says the L<small>ORD</small>, who has compassion on you"*
(Isaiah 54:10, NIV).

Additional Scripture and Promises

Deut. 7:13
Deut. 23:5
2 Chron. 30:9
Ps. 31:21
Ps. 32:10
Ps. 36:7
Ps. 57:3
Ps. 59:16, 17

Ps. 86:5, 15
Ps. 89:1, 2
Ps. 103:11–13
Ps. 116:5, 6
Ps. 146:8
Isa. 30:18
Isa. 49:10
Isa. 54:10

Isa. 63:9
Jer. 31:3
Lam. 3:22, 23
John 3:16
Rom. 5:5, 8
Rom. 8:35–39
Gal. 2:20

GOSSIP

DEAR LORD,

Why is it that I say things that get me into trouble and end up hurting others? I know gossiping is wrong because in Psalm 34:13 You've warned me to keep my tongue from evil. You have made it very clear in Psalm 52:2 that the tongue devises destruction and is like a sharp razor working deceitfully. In fact, in 1 Peter 4:15 You have included the wrong use of the tongue in the same category as the sins of a murderer and a thief! I don't want to be a gossiper!

So "Set a watch, O LORD, before my mouth" (KJV), as Psalm 141:3 says. I realize that my very salvation is at stake, for You say in Matthew 12:36 and 37 that I'll have to give an account on the day of judgment for every careless word I have spoken. For by my words I will be acquitted, and by my words I will be condemned.

Father God, I am praying the prayer that David prayed in Psalm 19:14: "Let the words of my mouth, and the meditation of my heart, be acceptable in thy sight, O LORD, my strength, and my redeemer" (KJV). I am trusting You to give me this victory. AMEN.

Promises About Gossip

"Keep your tongue from evil, And your lips from speaking deceit"
(Psalm 34:13, NKJV).

"Your tongue devises destruction,
Like a sharp razor, working deceitfully"
(Psalm 52:2, NKJV).

"But let none of you suffer as a murderer, a thief, an evildoer, or
as a busybody in other people's matters" (1 Peter 4:15, NKJV).

"Set a watch, O LORD, before my mouth" (Psalm 141:3, KJV).

" 'But I tell you that men will have to give account on the day of
judgment for every careless word they have spoken. For by your
words you will be acquitted, and by your words you will be
condemned' " (Matthew 12:36, 37, NIV).

"Let the words of my mouth, and the meditation of my heart,
be acceptable in thy sight, O LORD,
my strength, and my redeemer" (Psalm 19:14, KJV).

Additional Scripture and Promises

Exod. 20:16	*Prov. 10:19*	*Prov. 19:9*
Lev. 19:16	*Prov. 11:13*	*Prov. 20:15, 19*
Job 27:3, 4	*Prov. 12:18–20*	*Prov. 21:23*
Ps. 17:4	*Prov. 13:3*	*Prov. 26:20–22*
Ps. 34:13	*Prov. 15:4*	*James 3:6–8, 10, 11*
Ps. 52:2	*Prov. 16:24, 27, 28*	*James 3:17*
Prov. 3:29	*Prov. 17:28*	
Prov. 6:16–19	*Prov. 18:7, 8, 13, 21*	

GRIEF

My Precious Lord,

I feel so numb and empty and am overcome with grief. I know that my loved one is gone from this earth, yet my mind refuses to accept it. My eyes are swollen from crying—and it's hard to talk about my pain with anyone. Only You can understand the ache of losing someone so precious. Psalm 56:8 says, "You keep track of all my sorrows" (NLT). Not even my tears are wasted, for "You have collected all my tears in your bottle" (NLT).

Only You can understand the agony I'm feeling right now. My heart is broken, and I feel that I can't go on! *Please help me!* You have promised me in Psalm 34:18 that You are close to the brokenhearted and save those who are crushed in spirit. Jesus, save me! I find hope in Your promise in Revelation 21:4 that You will wipe away all my tears from my eyes and that at last there will be no more death, sorrow, or crying—neither will there be any more pain.

Oh, I can't wait for You to come in the clouds of glory and take me home. I'm so homesick for heaven! Thank You for Your promise in Matthew 5:4: "Blessed are they that mourn: for they shall be comforted" (KJV). Oh Father, hold me in Your arms and let me feel Your comforting presence. I ask everything in the name of Jesus who loves me. Amen.

PROMISES ABOUT GRIEF

"You keep track of all my sorrows. You have collected all my tears in your bottle. You have recorded each one in your book"
(Psalm 56:8, NLT).

"The LORD is close to the brokenhearted and saves those who are crushed in spirit"
(Psalm 34:18, NIV).

"And God shall wipe away all tears from their eyes; and there shall be no more death, neither sorrow, nor crying, neither shall there be any more pain: for the former things are passed away"
(Revelation 21:4, KJV).

"Blessed are they that mourn: for they shall be comforted"
(Matthew 5:4, KJV).

ADDITIONAL SCRIPTURE AND PROMISES

Isa. 25:8	*Isa. 61:1–3*	*Matt. 5:4*
Isa. 30:19	*Isa. 65:17–19*	*Matt. 11:28*
Isa. 35:10	*Isa. 66:13*	*Luke 6:21*
Isa. 41:10	*Ps. 23:4*	*Rom. 8:18, 28*
Isa. 43:2	*Ps. 30:5*	*2 Cor. 12:9*
Isa. 49:13	*Ps. 42:11*	*2 Cor. 1:3, 4*
Isa. 51:11	*Ps. 69:20*	*1 Pet. 4:12, 13, 19*
Isa. 53:3, 4	*Ps. 103:13*	*1 Pet. 5:7*

GUIDANCE

PRECIOUS LORD,

I come to you seeking guidance in my life, for I need to know which direction You want me to go. I've done things my own way before and suffered the consequences. I don't want to walk down that path again.

In Proverbs 3:6 You admonish me not to depend on my own understanding, but to seek Your will and ask You to direct my paths. So Lord, I'm not just asking, I'm pleading! Please show me what You want me to do. I don't know what's ahead, but You do. I'm claiming Your promise in Isaiah 30:21 that whether I turn to the right or left, You'll tell me, " 'This is the way; walk in it' " (NIV). And when I can't quite hear Your voice, Psalm 119:105 reminds me that "Your word is a lamp to my feet and a light for my path" (NIV).

I claim Your promise in Psalm 32:8 that You will instruct me, teach me the way to go, counsel me, and watch over me. It gives me so much courage and comfort to know that You are guiding me each step I take. Thank You, Father, for leading me with Your unfailing love and faithfulness, as You've promised to do in Psalm 25:9. I'm ready, now, for Your marching orders. It's going to be a good day! I can't wait to see what You have planned for me! Thank You, Jesus. AMEN.

Promises About Guidance

"*Trust in the LORD with all your heart; do not depend on your own understanding. Seek his will in all you do, and he will show you which path to take*" (Proverbs 3:6, NLT).

"*Whether you turn to the right or to the left, your ears will hear a voice behind you, saying, 'This is the way; walk in it'*" (Isaiah 30:21, NIV).

"*Your word is a lamp to my feet And a light to my path*" (Psalm 119:105, NKJV).

"*I will instruct you and teach you in the way you should go; I will counsel you and watch over you*" (Psalm 32:8, NIV).

"*The LORD is good and does what is right; he shows the proper path to those who go astray. He leads the humble in doing right, teaching them his way. The LORD leads with unfailing love and faithfulness all who keep his covenant and obey his demands*" (Psalm 25:8–10, NLT).

Additional Scripture and Promises

Ps. 16:7, 8, 11
Ps. 19:7–11
Ps. 23
Ps. 25:9
Ps. 32:8
Ps. 37:23
Ps. 48:14
Ps. 73:23, 24

Ps. 143:10
Prov. 3:5–7
Prov. 4:11–13
Prov. 13:20
Prov. 16:9
Prov. 19:20, 21
Isa. 30:21
Isa. 42:16

Micah 6:8
John 8:12, 31, 32
John 14:16, 17
John 16:13
James 1:5
James 1:25

GUILT

DEAR FATHER IN HEAVEN,

My heart is heavy with this burden of guilt that I can't seem to shake. I am so sorry for my sins. As You know, I have repented and claimed Your promise in 1 John 1:9 that if I confess my sins, You are faithful and just to forgive me my sins and to cleanse me from all unrighteousness. Jeremiah 31:34 says that You will not only forgive my iniquity, but that You will remember my sins no more!

Yet Satan keeps reminding me of my past sins, and once again I'm flooded with guilt! Thank You for the reassurance in 1 John 3:20 that even if I feel condemned in my heart, You are greater and know everything. I'm claiming Hebrews 10:22 as my weapon against the devil. Praise God that I have a great High Priest so I can go right into the presence of God, with an honest heart fully trusting Him. For my guilty conscience has been sprinkled with Christ's blood to make me clean.

Without wavering, I will hold tightly to the hope I have, *for You, God, can be trusted to keep Your promise.* Lord, I rejoice that You have made me holy and blameless. And I shout like David did in Psalm 32:5, "All my guilt is gone" (NLT)! Hallelujah. AMEN.

PROMISES ABOUT GUILT

"If we confess our sins, He is faithful and just to forgive us our sins and to cleanse us from all unrighteousness" (1 John 1:9, NKJV).

"For I will forgive their iniquity, and I will remember their sin no more" (Jeremiah 31:34, KJV).

"For if our heart condemn us, God is greater than our heart, and knoweth all things" (1 John 3:20, KJV).

"Let us draw near to God with a sincere heart in full assurance of faith, having our hearts sprinkled to cleanse us from a guilty conscience and having our bodies washed with pure water" (Hebrews 10:22, NIV).

"Finally, I confessed all my sins to you and stopped trying to hide my guilt. I said to myself, 'I will confess my rebellion to the LORD.' And you forgave me! All my guilt is gone" (Psalm 32:5, NLT).

ADDITIONAL SCRIPTURE AND PROMISES

Ps. 37:27	*Luke 15:10*	*Col. 1:13, 14*
Ps. 51:10	*Acts 3:19, 20*	*Heb. 8:12*
Ps. 103:12	*Rom. 3:23, 24*	*1 Pet. 1:18–21*
Ps. 111:1, 9	*Rom. 8:1-3*	*1 John 1:7*
Isa. 55:7	*2 Cor. 5:17*	*1 John 2:1, 12*
Jer. 33:8	*2 Cor. 7:10*	
Ezek. 18:21	*Eph. 5:25–27*	

HAPPINESS

DEAR LOVING, HEAVENLY FATHER,

There are so many bad things happening all around me. So much suffering, sickness, and death that sometimes it is hard for me to have the happiness in my heart that I know You want me to have. Oh Lord, Psalm 118:24 reminds me that I am so blessed. Because of all You have done for me, I can choose to be happy regardless of what happens.

Father God, You are the Source of all happiness. Psalm 4:7 says that You put gladness in my heart. Psalm 16:8 and 9 reminds me that just keeping close to You makes my heart glad. Oh Lord, please stay close to me!

I treasure Your words in Ecclesiastes 5:19, 20 that when I accept whatever comes to me and am happy in my work, You will keep me so occupied with gladness of heart that I won't have time to reflect on negative things that have happened—or that might happen. That's what I want for my life.

I claim the happiness and gladness of heart that You have promised in Proverbs 15:13. Thank You for putting a song in my heart and a smile on my face! I love You, Jesus. AMEN.

Promises About Happiness

"This is the day the LORD has made;
let us rejoice and be glad in it"
(Psalm 118:24, NIV).

"Thou hast put gladness in my heart"
(Psalm 4:7, KJV).

"I have set the LORD always before me: . . .
Therefore my heart is glad"
(Psalm 16:8, 9, KJV).

"When God gives any man wealth and possessions, and enables
him to enjoy them, to accept his lot and be happy in his
work—this is a gift of God. He seldom reflects on the days of his
life, because God keeps him occupied with gladness of heart"
(Ecclesiastes 5:19, 20, NIV).

"A happy heart makes the face cheerful,
but heartache crushes the spirit"
(Proverbs 15:13, NIV).

Additional Scripture and Promises

Job 5:17	*Prov. 14:21*	*Eccles. 9:7*
Ps. 5:11	*Prov. 15:13*	*John 16:33*
Ps. 64:10	*Prov. 16:20*	*Rom. 14:22*
Ps. 68:3	*Prov. 28:14*	*Gal. 5:22*
Ps. 90:15	*Prov. 29:18*	*Phil. 4:4*
Ps. 104:34	*Eccles. 2:24–26*	*James 5:11, 13*
Ps. 144:15	*Eccles. 3:4*	*1 Pet. 3:14*
Prov. 3:13	*Eccles. 8:15*	*1 Pet. 4:14*

HEALING

My Father in Heaven,

I kneel before Your presence asking for healing in my life. I claim Your promise in James 5:15 that "the prayer offered in faith will make the sick person well; the Lord will raise him up" (NIV). Oh Lord, I am praying with faith, knowing that You are the greatest Physician of all and that You alone have the power to heal. I feel so broken inside, but You have promised me in Psalm 23:3 that You will restore my soul. And in Jeremiah 30:17 You have said, " ' "I will restore you to health and heal your wounds" ' " (NIV).

I pray the prayer of David in Psalm 103:2 and 3: "Bless the LORD, O my soul, . . . Who heals all your diseases" (NKJV). I know that I am asking for a miracle of healing just as You healed the sick in Bible times. You have said in Matthew 7:7 that if I ask, I will receive. So, I come to You asking that I be fully restored so I may serve You and my life will glorify You. But, more importantly, I ask that Your will be done.

I just want to be in Your plan for my life, and whatever that is, I accept Your will joyfully, knowing that You love me more than anyone else and want only what is best for me. I thank You in advance for whatever Your plan may be. AMEN.

Promises About Healing

"And the prayer offered in faith will make the sick person well;
the Lord will raise him up. If he has sinned, he will be forgiven"
(James 5:15, NIV).

"He restores my soul; He leads me in the paths of righteousness
for His name's sake" (Psalm 23:3, NKJV).

" ' "I will restore you to health and heal your wounds,"
declares the LORD, "because you are called an outcast,
Zion for whom no one cares" ' " (Jeremiah 30:17, NIV).

"Bless the LORD, O my soul, And forget not all His benefits: Who
forgives all your iniquities, Who heals all your diseases"
(Psalm 103:2, 3, NKJV).

" 'Ask, and it will be given to you; seek, and you will find;
knock, and it will be opened to you' " (Matthew 7:7, NKJV).

Additional Scripture and Promises

2 Kings 4:32–37
2 Kings 5:10–14
2 Chron. 7:14
Ps. 6:2
Ps. 30:2, 3
Ps. 41:3
Ps. 71:20, 21
Ps. 103:1–5

Prov. 17:22
Isa. 53:4, 5
Isa. 58:8
Mal. 4:2
Matt. 8:5–13
Matt. 9:1–8, 18–31, 35
Matt. 12:10–13, 22, 23
Matt. 20:30–34

Mark 1:23–34, 40–42
Mark 7:31–37
Luke 9:11
Luke 17:11–19
John 5:1–9
John 11:38–44
Acts 14:8–10
Acts 28:8

HONESTY

DEAR FATHER GOD,

I am struggling today with being honest, telling myself that it's OK to tell "a little white lie," but I know in my heart there is no such thing. A lie is a lie. But do I have to tell the whole truth?

I know people who believe Satan's lie that there's nothing wrong with a little dishonesty—as long as you don't get caught! While You, Jesus, say in John 14:6 that You are the Way, *the Truth,* and the Life. I want to be like You! I want to walk honestly and to keep Your law as given in Leviticus 19:11, 12 to " ' "not steal, nor deal falsely, nor lie to one another" ' " (NKJV).

May Proverbs 16:8 be my motto: it's better to be poor and godly than rich and dishonest. I claim Your promise in Isaiah 33:15, 16 that if I walk righteously and speak what is right, You'll protect and provide for me. Lord, You know my heart. You know I want to be honest in the sight of all men, so I claim Your promise in Psalm 51:5–7 that You will teach me how—and that when I fail, You will purify me from my sins so I will be whiter than snow.

Thank You for helping me stand firm as Ephesians 6:14 says, with the belt of truth buckled around my waist and the breastplate of righteousness in place! In Your precious holy name I pray. AMEN.

Promises About Honesty

"Jesus answered, 'I am the way and the truth and the life' "
(John 14:6, NIV).

*" ' "You shall not steal, nor deal falsely, nor lie to one another.
And you shall not swear by My name falsely, nor shall you
profane the name of your God: I am the LORD" ' "*
(Leviticus 19:11, 12, NKJV).

*"Better to have little, with godliness, than to be rich and
dishonest" (Proverbs 16:8, NLT).*

*"He who walks righteously and speaks what is right, . . . this is
the man who will dwell on the heights, whose refuge will be the
mountain fortress. His bread will be supplied, and water will
not fail him" (Isaiah 33:15, 16, NIV).*

*"You desire honesty from the womb, teaching me wisdom even
there" (Psalm 51:6, NLT).*

*"Stand firm then, with the belt of truth buckled around
your waist, with the breastplate of righteousness in place"
(Ephesians 6:14, NIV).*

Additional Scripture and Promises

Ps. 34:12, 13	Prov. 16:8, 13	1 Cor. 13:6
Ps. 37:21	Prov. 21:23	2 Cor. 8:21
Ps. 119:28	Prov. 28:24	2 Cor. 13:7
Prov. 10:9	Isa. 28:15	Gal. 6:9
Prov. 11:1	Jer. 48:10	Eph. 4:29
Prov. 12:17, 19–22	Zech. 8:17	Phil. 4:8
Prov. 13:5	Luke 20:25	2 Tim. 2:15
Prov. 14:8	Rom. 13:7, 8	1 Pet. 4:11

HOPE

PRECIOUS HEAVENLY FATHER,

My burdens are so heavy that at times my life seems hopeless. Why even bother to go on? But then I think of the eagles soaring in the sky—so graceful, so beautiful—and Your promise in Isaiah 40:31 comes to mind: "Those who hope in the LORD will renew their strength. They will soar on wings like eagles; they will run and not grow weary, they will walk and not be faint" (NIV). Thank You, Lord, for reminding me that with You there is always hope!

Even in the middle of Lamentations, the book of weeping, You placed a gem of hope. Lamentations 3:21–24 says, "Yet I still dare to hope when I remember this: The faithful love of the LORD never ends! His mercies never cease. Great is his faithfulness; his mercies begin afresh each morning" (NLT).

And I'm reassured by Your promise in Jeremiah 29:11, " 'For I know the plans I have for you, . . . plans to prosper you and . . . to give you hope and a future' " (NIV). Wow! What a promise! The future I'm looking forward to is the blessed hope of eternal life!

Help me to share Your hope and love with others while patiently waiting for You to come back and take us home to live with You forever. Oh, I can't wait for that glorious day! In Jesus' name I claim all that You have promised. AMEN.

Promises About Hope

"Those who hope in the LORD will renew their strength.
They will soar on wings like eagles; they will run
and not grow weary, they will walk and not be faint"
(Isaiah 40:31, NIV).

"Yet I still dare to hope when I remember this:
The faithful love of the LORD never ends!
His mercies never cease. Great is his faithfulness; his mercies
begin afresh each morning.
I say to myself, 'The LORD is my inheritance; therefore,
I will hope in him!' " (Lamentations 3:21–24, NLT).

" 'For I know the plans I have for you,' declares the LORD,
'plans to prosper you and not to harm you,
plans to give you hope and a future' "
(Jeremiah 29:11, NIV).

Additional Scripture and Promises

Ps. 30:5	*Micah 7:7*	*1 Thess. 2:19*
Ps. 33:18, 22	*John 16:33*	*1 Thess. 4:13*
Ps. 38:15	*Rom. 5:2, 5*	*1 Thess. 5:8*
Ps. 42:5, 6	*Rom. 8:24, 25*	*Heb. 3:6*
Ps. 71:5, 6, 14	*1 Cor. 15:19*	*Heb. 6:11, 18, 19*
Isa. 38:18	*2 Cor. 1:22*	*Heb. 10:23*
Isa. 40:31	*Eph. 1:18*	*1 Pet. 1:3, 13*
Jer. 17:7, 13, 17	*Col. 1:23, 27*	*1 John 3:2, 3, 24*

HOSPITALITY

Dear Loving Savior,

I come to You asking for the gift of hospitality because I realize I am lacking in this area of my life. Yet this is something You have commanded me to do. Lord, I want to be like You. I want to be able to open my home to others that You may minister to their needs through me as Romans 12:13 says I should do. But I need Your help.

You have made it very clear how much You value giving to others. I have read in Matthew 19:21 Your response to the rich young ruler's question about what he needed to do to be saved. You told him that he should sell his possessions and give the money to the poor.

Oh Lord, I'm convicted that if this is Your standard for judging whether my love for You is the real thing or just lip service, I would fall short! Forgive me for selfishly living my life without going out of my comfort zone to open my home to those who need lodging or to strangers needing a good meal. It's hard enough for me to invite friends over, but I seldom think of the poor, crippled, lame, and blind, as You say I should in Luke 14:12–14. *Lord, change me!*

Place within my heart Your gift of hospitality! Give me a heart that aches for those in need, and help me to remember as I'm entertaining them that as Hebrews 13:1, 2 says, I might be entertaining angels—or You! Amen.

Promises About Hospitality

"When God's people are in need, be ready to help them. Always be eager to practice hospitality" (Romans 12:13, NLT).

" 'If you want to be perfect, go, sell what you have and give to the poor, and you will have treasure in heaven; and come, follow Me' " (Matthew 19:21, NKJV).

"Jesus said to his host, . . . 'when you give a banquet, invite the poor, the crippled, the lame, the blind, and you will be blessed. Although they cannot repay you, you will be repaid at the resurrection of the righteous' " (Luke 14:12–14, NIV).

*"Let brotherly love continue.
Do not forget to entertain strangers, for by so doing some have unwittingly entertained angels"*
(Hebrews 13:1, 2, NKJV).

Additional Scripture and Promises

Ps. 82:3	*Matt. 10:42*	*Acts 3:6*
Prov. 3:27, 28	*Matt. 19:21*	*Acts 20:35*
Prov. 14:21, 31	*Matt. 25:34–36, 40*	*Rom. 15:1–3*
Prov. 19:17	*Mark 9:37*	*2 Cor. 11:9*
Prov. 25:21, 22	*Luke 3:11*	*Gal. 2:10*
Prov. 31:9	*Luke 6:27, 36–38*	*Gal. 5:14*
Isa. 58:7, 8	*Luke 10:30–34*	*1 Thess. 5:14*
Zech. 7:9, 10, 13	*Luke 11:8*	*James 1:27*

HUMILITY

PRECIOUS JESUS,

You know my heart and the pride issues I struggle with. I like being right and feel defensive when someone doesn't appreciate all I do. It makes me feel good when others praise my efforts, but I cringe when I am criticized or told that I haven't done something right. Lord, please cleanse me and give me a new heart like Your heart. Take my selfish pride and make me humble like You.

I claim Your promise in James 4:10 that You will lift me up if I humble myself before You. My greatest desire is to fully reflect You in all that I do. Please keep me humble so I may claim Your promise in Psalm 149:4 and receive Your crown of salvation! The journey on this earth is difficult, and I am longing to spend eternity with You. I have learned in Psalm 25:9 that if I am humble, You will teach me what is right and the way I should go, so that I may someday have a home in heaven.

I realize that You cannot teach a proud heart, so precious Father, keep me grounded and close to You. And may Micah 6:8 always be my guide—that I may do justly, love mercy, and walk humbly with You forever. Thank You for hearing and answering my prayers. AMEN.

Promises About Humility

*"Humble yourselves before the Lord,
and he will lift you up" (James 4:10, NIV).*

*"The LORD takes delight in his people; he crowns the humble
with salvation" (Psalm 149:4, NIV).*

*"He guides the humble in what is right and teaches them his
way" (Psalm 25:9, NIV).*

*"He has shown you, O man, what is good; And what does the
LORD require of you But to do justly, To love mercy, And to walk
humbly with your God?" (Micah 6:8, NKJV).*

Additional Scripture and Promises

2 Sam. 22:28	Prov. 15:33	Matt. 18:4
Ps. 9:12	Prov. 16:18, 19	Matt. 23:11, 12
Ps. 10:17	Prov. 18:12	Rom. 12:3
Ps. 25:9	Prov. 22:4	Eph. 4:1, 2
Ps. 147:6	Prov. 29:23	Phil. 2:3, 5–8
Ps. 149:4	Isa. 5:15	Titus 3:2
Prov. 3:34	Isa. 57:15	James 4:6, 10
Prov. 11:2	Matt. 11:29	1 Pet. 5:5–7

IDENTITY

Dear Loving, Heavenly Father,

Thank You for making it clear that *who* I am is not dependent on my family's reputation, the status of my friends, the prestige of my job, or the success of my accomplishments. Others may look down on me because I don't have worldly honor and recognition. But Lord, I claim the promise in 1 John 3:1 that regardless of what people think of me, I belong to You—the God of the universe! I'm Your child.

You know me personally. Isaiah 43:1 tells me that You call me by name. In Isaiah 49:16, You say that You've engraved me on the palms of Your hands. And in Matthew 10:30, You say You even know how many hairs I have on my head!

Dear Lord, when I'm tempted to question whether I'm worthy of such lavish love, I claim Your promise in Romans 8:16, 17 that Your Spirit will testify to me that I am Your child, and therefore Your heir and a co-heir with Christ.

May I never forget the promise in Romans 14:8 that in whatever circumstance of life I find myself, my identity is in You. Amen.

Promises About Identity

"How great is the love the Father has lavished on us, that we should be called children of God! And that is what we are!" (1 John 3:1, NIV).

"This is what the LORD says . . . 'Fear not, for I have redeemed you; I have summoned you by name; you are mine' " (Isaiah 43:1, NIV).

"This is what the LORD says: . . . 'See, I have engraved you on the palms of my hands' " (Isaiah 49:8, 16, NIV).

"The Spirit himself testifies with our spirit that we are God's children. Now if we are children, then we are heirs—heirs of God and co-heirs with Christ, if indeed we share in his sufferings in order that we may also share in his glory" (Romans 8:16, 17, NIV).

"If we live, we live to the Lord; and if we die, we die to the Lord. So, whether we live or die, we belong to the Lord" (Romans 14:8, NIV).

Additional Scripture and Promises

Gen. 2:7	John 15:5–8, 15	2 Cor. 6:18
Gen. 5:1	Acts 17:28	Gal. 3:26–29
Ps. 8:4-9	Rom. 8:14–17	Eph. 1:3–6, 18, 19
Ps. 100:3	1 Cor. 3:16	Eph. 2:10, 19–22
Ps. 139:1–6, 13–16	1 Cor. 12:27	Col. 3:4
Prov. 31:29–31	2 Cor. 3:3	1 Thess. 5:5
Jer. 1:5	2 Cor. 5:17, 20	1 Pet. 2:9
Luke 12:6, 7	2 Cor. 6:16	1 John 3:1

INTEGRITY

PRECIOUS LORD,

You showed what true integrity is when You were crucified on the cross for those who not only rejected You, but beat You, lied about You, and spit on You. When You breathed Your last breath, it was with peace and assurance on Your face. There were no angry words of defense, no last cutting remarks—only forgiveness in Your heart for those who had mistreated You. Your whole life is an example that I long to follow. Oh Lord, I want my life to reflect Your character.

You have said in Proverbs 16:7 that when my ways are pleasing to You, You make even my enemies live at peace with me. Help me to live today—and everyday—in an upright manner which You would be proud of, so that I may experience the peace and rest that You have promised in Isaiah 57:2.

I want my life to be one of integrity so that when You search my heart and examine my mind, as You say You will do in Jeremiah 17:10, You can reward me according to my conduct.

I love Your promise in Psalm 41:12 that "In my integrity you uphold me and set me in your presence forever" (NIV)! I pray that You will keep me ever honest and true to You. AMEN.

Promises About Integrity

*"When a man's ways are pleasing to the L*ORD,
He makes even his enemies to be at peace with him"
(Proverbs 16:7, NKJV).

"Those who walk uprightly enter into peace;
they find rest as they lie in death"
(Isaiah 57:2, NIV).

*" 'I the L*ORD *search the heart and examine the mind,*
to reward a man according to his conduct,
according to what his deeds deserve' "
(Jeremiah 17:10, NIV).

"In my integrity you uphold me and
set me in your presence forever"
(Psalm 41:12, NIV).

Additional Scripture and Promises

Job 2:3, 9	Prov. 2:7, 8	Gal. 6:7, 8
Job 31:6	Prov. 10:9	1 Thess. 5:23, 24
Ps. 7:8	Prov. 11:3	1 Tim. 3:13
Ps. 25:21	Prov. 13:6	2 Tim. 4:7, 8
Ps. 26:1	Prov. 20:7	James 5:16
Ps. 41:12	Luke 16:10	1 Pet. 3:12
Ps. 84:11	Rom. 2:6, 7	1 John 2:17

JEALOUSY

My Loving, Heavenly Father,

I come before You claiming the blood of my Savior to free me from my coldness toward those who are jealous of me. I'm consumed with how they treat me and keep replaying all the hurt and rejection over in my mind. You had so many people jealous of Your own Son, yet You still gave Him to die for our sins. Please give me Your victory and help me to treat those who show jealousy toward me with Your love, as You would have me to do.

I long for Your peace that gives life to my body and soul, as You have promised to give me in Proverbs 14:30. I know the sting of a jealous tongue. I don't want to do the same to someone else. That is why I also ask, Lord, that You remove any envy in my heart that I may have toward others. I don't want to keep letting the envy of others rot my bones. I cling to You, my God, and look to You for deliverance.

In Galatians 5:26, You have warned me not to become conceited, envying others. And James 3:16 tells me, "For where envy and self-seeking exist, confusion and every evil are there" (NKJV). You have made it very clear in Ephesians 5:5 that jealousy and covetousness will keep me out of the kingdom!

Please remove anything from my heart that would separate me from You. More than anything, precious Father, I long to be close to You. Thank You for Your peace that floods my soul. AMEN.

Promises About Jealousy

"A heart at peace gives life to the body,
but envy rots the bones"
(Proverbs 14:30, NIV).

"Let us not become conceited,
provoking one another, envying one another"
(Galatians 5:26, NKJV).

"For where envy and self-seeking exist,
confusion and every evil thing are there"
(James 3:16, NKJV).

"For this you know, that no fornicator,
unclean person, or covetous man, who is an idolater,
has any inheritance in the kingdom of Christ and God"
(Ephesians 5:5, NKJV).

Additional Scripture and Promises

Exod. 20:17	*Prov. 21:26*	*Luke 12:15, 22, 23*
Ps. 37:1, 7	*Prov. 24:1, 19*	*Rom. 7:7*
Ps. 49:16, 17	*Eccles. 4:4*	*Rom. 13:13*
Ps. 119:36	*Isa. 26:11*	*1 Cor. 3:3*
Prov. 3:31	*Matt. 16:26*	
Prov. 14:30	*Mark 7:21, 22*	

Joy

Precious Heavenly Father,

This world is filled with heartache and pain all around me, and sometimes it is hard for me to be joyful. I long for the joy only You can give. I know I can choose to be content—even happy. But I also know real joy is a gift from You. Psalm 5:11 says that joy comes as a result of trusting You and loving Your name; and John 15:11 and 12 points to obedience to Your commandment to love others as a source of joy.

Oh Lord, I desire Your gift of joy, and I pray that You will help me live in such a way that joy will be my constant companion. Psalm 16:11 tells me that "In Your presence is fullness of joy" (NKJV). I realize that this promise is conditional on me choosing to spend time each day talking to You and reading Your Word. That's why I pray the prayer found in Psalm 90:14: "Satisfy [me] in the morning with your unfailing love, that [I] may sing for joy and be glad all [my] days" (NIV).

In John 16:24, You say, " 'Ask and you will receive, and your joy will be complete' " (NIV). I know what You say is true, because each time a miracle comes my way or I experience a divine appointment, I explode with joy! Thank You, thank You, dear Lord, for Your precious gift of joy. Amen.

Promises About Joy

"But let all those that put their trust in thee rejoice: let them ever shout for joy, because thou defendest them: let them also that love thy name be joyful in thee" (Psalm 5:11, KJV).

"These things have I spoken unto you, that my joy might remain in you, and that your joy might be full. This is my commandment, That ye love one another, as I have loved you" (John 15:11, 12, KJV).

"You will show me the path of life; In Your presence is fullness of joy; At Your right hand are pleasures forevermore" (Psalm 16:11, NKJV).

"Satisfy us in the morning with your unfailing love, that we may sing for joy and be glad all our days" (Psalm 90:14, NIV).

Jesus said, " 'Until now you have not asked for anything in my name. Ask and you will receive, and your joy will be complete' " (John 16:24, NIV).

Additional Scripture and Promises

Deut. 16:15	*Ps. 97:11*	*Isa. 51:11*
Ps. 5:11	*Ps. 100*	*Jer. 31:1*
Ps. 19:8	*Ps. 118:24*	*Luke 10:20, 21*
Ps. 30:5, 11, 12	*Ps. 119:111*	*John 15:7, 9–11*
Ps. 33:1	*Ps. 126:2–6*	*Rom. 15:13, 32*
Ps. 35:9	*Ps. 149:5*	*Gal. 5:22*
Ps. 51:8, 12, 13	*Prov. 17:21, 22*	*Phil. 4:4*
Ps. 68:3	*Isa. 29:19*	*Jude 24, 25*

JUDGING

PRECIOUS LORD,

I'm tired of the coldness in my heart toward others. I find myself judging people harshly, and it's hard for me to accept the value You have placed on them. When I look at Calvary and read in Luke 23:33 and 34 how You didn't judge even those who nailed You to the cross, but cried out to Your heavenly Father to forgive them because they didn't know what they were doing, I'm so ashamed. I confess that my judging comes from a selfish heart. Please empty me of self and forgive me for not treating others like You treat me. I claim the new heart and spirit You have promised me in Ezekiel 36:26 and 27.

Help me to remember Your counsel in Matthew 7:1 and 2 not to judge, because I will be judged in the same way! John 8:7 tells me that when the woman caught in adultery was brought before You, You said, " 'If any one of you is without sin, let him be the first to throw a stone at her' " (NIV). Oh Father, I am a sinner and have no right to pass judgment on anyone!

In Matthew 7:5, You tell me clearly that I must remove the plank from my own eye before removing the speck from my brother's eye. Please forgive me and fill my heart with Your love for everyone. And help me to honor You by letting You do the judging—for You are the only righteous Judge. AMEN.

Promises About Judging

"And when they had come to the place called Calvary, there they crucified Him, and the criminals, one on the right hand and the other on the left. Then Jesus said, 'Father, forgive them, for they do not know what they do'" (Luke 23:33, 34, NKJV).

"'I will give you a new heart and put a new spirit within you; I will take the heart of stone out of your flesh and give you a heart of flesh. I will put My Spirit within you and cause you to walk in My statutes, and you will keep My judgments and do them'" (Ezekiel 36:26, 27, NJKV).

"'Judge not, that you be not judged. For with what judgment you judge, you will be judged; and with the measure you use, it will be measured back to you'" (Matthew 7:1, 2, NKJV).

"'If any one of you is without sin, let him be the first to throw a stone at her'" (John 8:7, NIV).

"'You hypocrite, first take the plank out of your own eye, and then you will see clearly to remove the speck from your brother's eye'" (Matthew 7:5, NIV).

Additional Scripture and Promises

Lev. 19:15	Luke 9:49–55	1 Cor. 11:31
Prov. 17:15	John 7:24	2 Cor. 10:12
Prov. 30:10	John 8:7–11	Col. 2:16
Isa. 50:9	John 12:47	Titus 3:2
Zech. 7:9, 10	Rom. 2:1	James 4:11
Matt. 7:1–5	Rom. 14:4, 10–13	1 Pet. 3:16
Matt. 12:37	1 Cor. 4:3–5	
Luke 3:14	1 Cor. 6:2–5	

JUSTICE

Dear Mighty God and King,

I praise You for who You are, the all knowing, fair, and just God, the King of the universe. I proclaim Your name and ascribe greatness to You, O God. You are the Rock; Your work is perfect; all Your ways are justice. You are a God of truth and justice. Righteous and upright are You. Lord, I desire to be just and upright like You. Micah 6:8 tells me that You don't require sacrifice. You just ask that I live justly, love mercy, and walk humbly before You.

You instruct me in Proverbs 31:8 and 9 that I should speak up for those who can't speak up for themselves; that I should defend the poor and judge fairly. In Isaiah 1:17, You tell me not only to encourage and seek justice for the oppressed, but also to defend the fatherless and the widow.

Lord, it's so easy to get caught up in the struggles of my own life that I don't take the time to help those who are being treated unjustly. Forgive me! Open my eyes to the needs of others and give me courage to plead for justice for all.

Now, Lord, I claim Your promises in Isaiah 30:18 and Psalm 11:7, that You, as a God of justice, will bless me and that if I am upright, I will see Your face. Thank You, God, for Your just and holy ways. Amen.

Promises About Justice

"He has shown you, O man, what is good; And what does the LORD require of you But to do justly, To love mercy, And to walk humbly with your God?" (Micah 6:8, NKJV).

" 'Speak up for those who cannot speak for themselves, for the rights of all who are destitute. Speak up and judge fairly; defend the rights of the poor and needy' " (Proverbs 31:8, 9, NIV).

" 'Learn to do right! Seek justice, encourage the oppressed. Defend the cause of the fatherless, plead the case of the widow' " (Isaiah 1:17, NIV).

"The LORD is a God of justice. Blessed are all who wait for him!" (Isaiah 30:18, NIV).

"For the LORD is righteous, he loves justice; upright men will see his face" (Psalm 11:7, NIV).

Additional Scripture and Promises

Prov. 3:33	*Isa. 26:7*	*Rom. 7:12*
Prov. 4:18	*Isa. 30:18*	*Gal. 3:11*
Prov. 9:9	*Isa. 45:21*	*Phil. 4:8*
Prov. 11:9	*Hosea 14:9*	*Col. 4:1*
Prov. 12:13, 21	*Hab. 2:4*	*Heb. 2:2*
Prov. 20:7	*Matt. 5:45*	*Heb. 10:38*
Prov. 24:16	*Luke 14:14*	*1 John 1:9*
Prov. 29:26, 27	*Luke 15:7*	*Rev. 15:3*

KINDNESS

DEAR KIND, LOVING FATHER IN HEAVEN,

I'm so thankful for the awesome God that You are, so full of love and kindness, even when I disappoint You and make mistakes. I want to be like You. In 1 Thessalonians 5:15, You tell me I should never repay wrong with wrong. Instead, Romans 12:10 says I should be kindly affectionate to others and take delight in honoring them. Matthew 5:44 goes so far as to say that I should be kind to those who hate me! *Lord, how is this possible?*

My whole being seems to want to treat people as they have treated me—rather than following Your golden rule *to treat others as I would like to them treat me!* Ephesians 4:31, 32 tells me to get rid of feelings and actions that hurt others, such as bitterness, rage, harsh words, slander, and malicious behavior—and replace these with Christlike kindness, tenderheartedness, and forgiveness.

Oh Lord, give me the power and the determination to do this. And control me through the Holy Spirit so I will never hurt or abuse others. Instead, help me to always be kind. In Jesus' name I pray. AMEN.

Promises About Kindness

*"Make sure that nobody pays back wrong for wrong,
but always try to be kind to each other and to everyone else"*
(1 Thessalonians 5:15, NIV).

*"Be kindly affectionate to one another with brotherly love,
in honor giving preference to one another"*
(Romans 12:10, NKJV).

*" 'But I say to you, love your enemies,
bless those who curse you, do good to those who hate you,
and pray for those who spitefully use you and persecute you' "*
(Matthew 5:44, NKJV).

*"Get rid of all bitterness, rage, anger, harsh words, and slander,
as well as all types of evil behavior. Instead, be kind to each
other, tenderhearted, forgiving one another, just as God through
Christ has forgiven you"* (Ephesians 4:31, 32, NLT).

Additional Scripture and Promises

Deut. 22:1	Zech. 7:9	Col. 3:12
Ruth 3:10	Matt. 7:12	1 Thess. 5:15
Ps. 36:7	Luke 6:35	Titus 3:4, 5
Ps. 117:2	Rom. 12:10	Heb. 13:2
Prov. 11:16, 17	1 Cor. 13:4, 5	1 Pet. 3:8
Prov. 14:31	Gal. 5:22, 23	2 Pet. 1:5–7
Prov. 19:1	Gal. 6:2, 9, 10	1 John 3:17, 18
Jer. 31:3	Eph. 4:32	

LAZINESS

DEAR FATHER IN HEAVEN,

I realize I don't serve You the way I should. I could do so much more to witness for You. I always mean to, but I never seem to get around to it. I've never been an energetic person, but lately I've come to see myself as basically lazy, and I don't want to be that kind of person anymore. I have thought about what You said in Proverbs 13:4: "The soul of a lazy man desires, and has nothing; But the soul of the diligent shall be made rich" (NKJV).

I confess that I didn't think this applied to me until You opened my eyes to see my spiritual laziness. Please help me to get up early so that we can have uninterrupted time together. Forgive me for all the times I have ignored Your Holy Spirit's wake-up call. I don't want to be like the five virgins in Matthew 25 who were too lazy to put oil in their lamps, and missed out on the wedding. I also don't want to sleep during the harvest and cause the shame that You talk about in Proverbs 10:4 and 5. Please fill me with energy and a willingness to be used by You.

I'm claiming Your promise in Matthew 10:22 that " 'he who endures to the end will be saved' " (NKJV). Oh Lord, mold and make me into a worker who will endure to the end that I may receive Your heavenly reward! Remove all laziness within me. I want to start working for You right now, so please use me to be a blessing in someone's life today! In Jesus' name I pray. AMEN.

PROMISES ABOUT LAZINESS

"The soul of a lazy man desires, and has nothing;
But the soul of the diligent shall be made rich"
(Proverbs 13:4, NKJV).

" 'Then the kingdom of heaven shall be likened to ten virgins
who took their lamps and went out to meet the bridegroom.
Now five of them were wise, and five were foolish. Those who
were foolish took their lamps and took no oil with them' "
(Matthew 25:1–3, NKJV).

"He who has a slack hand becomes poor,
But the hand of the diligent makes rich.
He who gathers in summer is a wise son;
He who sleeps in harvest is a son who causes shame"
(Proverbs 10:4, 5, NKJV).

" 'And you will be hated by all for My name's sake.
But he who endures to the end will be saved' "
(Matthew 10:22, NKJV).

ADDITIONAL SCRIPTURE AND PROMISES

Prov. 12:11, 24   *Prov. 24:30–34*   *Eph. 4:28*
Prov. 13:4, 23   *Prov. 27:23, 27* *1 Thess. 4:11, 12*
Prov. 15:19   *Prov. 28:19*   *2 Thess. 3:10–12*
Prov. 20:13   *Eccles. 5:18, 19* *2 Tim. 2:6*
Prov. 21:5   *Rom. 12:11*

LEADERSHIP

PRECIOUS HEAVENLY FATHER,

You have trusted me with so much responsibility in this leadership position. Thank You for reminding me in 1 Peter 5:2–4 that You want me to direct those I'm responsible for as tenderly and patiently as You shepherd me. When I need to instruct or correct, may I do it with a spirit of love and mercy, for You are rich in mercy, and You loved me even when I was dead in sin (Ephesians 2:4, 5). Please make me willing to work side by side with others, ever cheering them on toward the goal of spending eternity with You.

Keep my eyes locked on You, for only then will they know that You are the true Leader. In 2 Samuel 23:3, You tell me that he who rules over men must be just. Lord, come into my heart and change me so that I will be a fair and just leader, always following Your voice. I lay hold of Your promise in Isaiah 41:10 that You will be my God, my help, my strength, and that You will uphold me with Your righteous right hand.

I pray the prayer in 2 Chronicles 1:10: Lord God, " 'Give me wisdom and knowledge, that I may lead' " as You would have me do. I love You and ask all these things in the name of Jesus who lives to intercede for me. AMEN.

Promises About Leadership

*"Be shepherds of God's flock that is under your care,
serving as overseers—not because you must, but because you are
willing, as God wants you to be; not greedy for money,
but eager to serve; not lording it over those entrusted to you,
but being examples to the flock. And when the Chief Shepherd
appears, you will receive the crown of glory that will never fade away"*
(1 Peter 5:2–4, NIV).

*" 'The God of Israel said, The Rock of Israel spoke to me:
"He who rules over men must be just, Ruling in the fear of God" ' "*
(2 Samuel 23:3, NKJV).

*" ' "Fear not, for I am with you; Be not be dismayed, for I am
your God. I will strengthen you, Yes, I will help you, I will
uphold you with My righteous right hand" ' "*
(Isaiah 41:10, NKJV).

" 'Give me wisdom and knowledge, that I may lead' "
(2 Chronicles 1:10, NIV).

*"But God, who is rich in mercy, for his great love
wherewith he loved us, Even when we were dead in sins"*
(Ephesians 2:4, 5, KJV).

Additional Scripture and Promises

2 Sam. 23:4	*John 13:3–5, 12–17*	*1 Tim. 3:1–12*
Prov. 8:12, 14–16	*Acts 1:8*	*2 Tim. 4:1–5*
Prov. 28:3	*Acts 14:23*	*Titus 1:5–9, 14*
Matt. 28:18–20	*Col. 2:9, 10*	*1 Pet. 5:2–4*

LONELINESS

DEAR FATHER IN HEAVEN,

I miss having friends and family around me. I understand why You said in Genesis 2:18 that it is not good to be alone. Matthew 18:20 suggests that even the effectiveness of prayer is enhanced when two or three are together. And Ecclesiastes 4:9 and 10 says that "Two are better than one" (NKJV) because if one falls down the other can help him up. But, Lord, I don't have anyone, so I call on You to fulfill Your promise in Psalm 68:5 and 6 that You'll be a Father to the fatherless, a Defender of widows, and that you'll set the lonely in families. That's me, Lord—*lonely!*

Romans 14:7 and 8 says that if we belong to You, none of us are ever alone. I keep telling myself that, but I need to feel Your presence more intimately. That's why I'm holding on to Your promise in Romans 8:39 that nothing will ever be able to separate me "from the love of God that is revealed in Christ Jesus our Lord" (NLT).

Oh precious heavenly Father, wrap Your arms around me and let me feel Your presence! Thank You for Your promises. I love You. AMEN.

Promises About Loneliness

"And the LORD God said, 'It is not good that man should be alone; I will make him a helper comparable to him' "
(Genesis 2:18, NKJV).

" 'Where two or three are gathered together in My name, I am there in the midst of them' " (Matthew 18:20, NKJV).

"Two are better than one, Because they have a good reward for their labor. For if they fall, one will lift up his companion"
(Ecclesiastes 4:9, 10, NKJV).

"A father of the fatherless, a defender of widows, is God in his holy dwelling. God sets the lonely in families" (Psalm 68:5, 6, NIV).

"None of us lives to himself alone and none of us dies to himself alone. If we live, we live to the Lord; and if we die, we die to the Lord. So, wither we live or die, we belong to the Lord"
(Romans 14:7, 8, NIV).

"No power in the sky above or in the earth below—indeed, nothing in all creation will ever be able to separate us from the love of God that is revealed in Christ Jesus our Lord"
(Romans 8:39, NLT).

Additional Scripture and Promises

Deut. 4:31	Isa. 26:3	2 Cor. 6:18
Deut. 31:6	Isa. 41:10	Eph. 2:19
1 Sam. 12:22	Isa. 58:9	Col. 2:10
Ps. 27:10	Hosea 2:19, 20	Heb. 13:5, 6
Ps. 40:17	Matt. 28:20	James 4:8
Ps. 73:23	John 14:1, 18–23, 27	1 Pet. 5:7
Ps. 145:18	John 15:4–7	Rev. 3:20
Ps. 147:3	1 Cor. 1:9	

LOVE

Dear Loving God,

Your compassionate love for people is so great, it's above comprehending. Thank You for loving me first, as 1 John 4:19 says. It's no wonder I love You so much. But I'm having trouble loving others as You have commanded us to do in Matthew 22:39. Oh Lord, I ask You to give me a compassionate heart for people. Some are so obnoxious, cruel, or repulsive; I just don't *feel* like loving them!

When You came to live on this earth You dealt with unloving people who ended up killing You, and yet You continued to love them supremely. Oh Lord, I want to be like You. In Ephesians 5:1 and 2, You say that we should be imitators of You. In Colossians 3:12–14, You tell us to clothe ourselves with compassion, kindness, humility, gentleness, and patience, "And over all of these virtues put on love, which binds them all together in perfect unity" (NIV). How is this possible?

You tell us in 1 John 4:12 that if we love others, You will live in us and make Your love complete in us. Oh loving Lord, I want to be Your "complete" compassionate *love* walking around in my shoes! Please come into my heart and live in me, because without You, it's almost impossible to truly love others. I praise You for who You are and for answering my prayer, in Jesus' name. Amen.

Promises About Love

"We love Him because He first loved us"
(1 John 4:19, NKJV).

"Be imitators of God, therefore, as dearly loved children
and live a life of love, just as Christ loved us and gave himself
up for us as a fragrant offering and sacrifice to God"
(Ephesians 5:1, 2, NIV).

"Therefore, as God's chosen people, holy and dearly loved,
clothe yourselves with compassion, kindness, humility,
gentleness and patience. Bear with each other and forgive
whatever grievances you may have against one another.
Forgive as the Lord forgave you. And over all these virtues
put on love, which binds them all together in perfect unity"
(Colossians 3:12–14, NIV).

"No one has ever seen God; but if we love one another,
God lives in us and his love is made complete in us"
(1 John 4:12, NIV).

Additional Scripture and Promises

Lev. 19:18	Rom. 12:9, 10	Heb. 13:1–2
Ps. 85:10	Rom. 13:8–10	James 2:8
Prov. 10:12	1 Cor. 13	1 Pet. 1:22
Prov. 17:9, 17	1 Cor. 16:14	1 Pet. 4:8
Matt. 5:44, 45	Eph. 4:2	1 John 2:10, 11
Mark 12:30–33	Phil. 2:3, 4	1 John 3:16–18, 23
Luke 6:27–31	Col. 3:12–14	1 John 4:7–21
John 15:9–14, 17	1 Thess. 3:12	1 John 5:2

LUST

Dear Father in Heaven,

I don't know what's happening to me, but I'm not the person I want to be. I'm fighting an intense battle over the control of my body and mind, and I'm so afraid I'm going to give in and that my sinful thoughts will become sinful actions. Please help me right now to overcome these passionate cravings that I'm experiencing. Oh Lord, bind the devil. Don't let my mind wander into his territory. I feel like Eve standing too close to the tree of knowledge of good and evil. I'm afraid I'm going to fall, unless I do exactly what You have said in James 4:7 that I should do: "Submit yourselves therefore to God. Resist the devil, and he will flee from you" (KJV).

Lord, thank You for that promise of victory. I submit myself—my whole body and soul—to You. And in faith, I see the devil running away. I claim Your promise in Romans 16:20 to crush him under my feet.

In Proverbs 6:25–28, I find gems of wisdom: "Do not lust in your heart . . . Can a man scoop fire into his lap without his clothes being burned? Can a man walk on hot coals without his feet being scorched?" (NIV). Lord, You have convicted me that if I really want to put lust out of my life, I have to control my senses—what I look at, hear, touch, taste, and smell.

Finally, I claim 1 Corinthians 10:13: "God is faithful; he will not let you be tempted beyond what you can bear" (NIV). I believe You will provide a way out so that I can stand up under any temptation. Thank You for Your promises. With You, I know I can be an overcomer. I praise You for the victory. Amen.

PROMISES ABOUT LUST

"Submit yourselves therefore to God.
Resist the devil, and he will flee from you"
(James 4:7, KJV).

"And the God of peace will crush Satan under your feet shortly"
(Romans 16:20, NKJV).

"Do not lust in your heart after her beauty or let her captivate
you with her eyes, for the prostitute reduces you to a loaf of
bread, and the adulteress preys upon your very life. Can a man
scoop fire into his lap without his clothes being burned? Can a
man walk on hot coals without his feet being scorched?"
(Proverbs 6:25–28, NIV).

"No temptation has seized you except what is common to man.
And God is faithful; he will not let you be tempted beyond what
you can bear. But when you are tempted, he will also provide a
way out so that you can stand up under it"
(1 Corinthians 10:13, NIV).

ADDITIONAL SCRIPTURE AND PROMISES

Prov. 6:25–29	1 Cor. 6:15–20	Heb. 4:15
Matt. 5:27, 28	2 Cor. 10:4	James 1:2–4, 13, 14
Matt. 6:13	Gal. 5:16, 17, 24	James 4:1–8
Matt. 18:8, 9	Eph. 2:3–6	1 Pet. 1:7, 14–16
Rom. 6:11–14	Eph. 4:22–24, 27	1 Pet. 2:11, 15–17
Rom. 8:37	Eph. 5:5–9, 18	1 Pet. 5:8, 9
Rom. 12:21	2 Tim. 2:22	2 Pet. 2:9
Rom. 13:14	Titus 2:11, 12	

LYING

DEAR FATHER GOD,

You are a God of truth, and my heart's desire is to be like You. I want to be as honest as the righteous 144,000 of whom Revelation 14:5 says they have no lies in their mouths. Yet sometimes I'm tempted to embellish the truth to make myself look better. And I'm ashamed to admit that sometimes blatant lies come out of my mouth! Oh Lord, forgive me! I know that Proverbs 6:16–19 says that two of the things You hate have to do with lying—a lying tongue and a false witness.

In Proverbs 12:22, You tell me that You detest lying lips, but that You delight in those who are truthful. I want You to be able to delight in me! So please, Father, touch my lips so that not a single lie will escape from my mouth. I'm pleading with You to remove all sin within me and fill me with Your presence that only Your goodness and truthfulness will shine out of me!

Don't let me stretch the truth when I talk about someone or when I make a report. I ask You to help me make my words so filled with truth that they will be like the choice silver mentioned in Proverbs 10:20. Thank You for answering my prayer. AMEN.

PROMISES ABOUT LYING

"Then I looked, and there before me was the Lamb, standing on Mount Zion, and with him 144,000 who had his name and his Father's name written on their foreheads. . . . No lie was found in their mouths; they are blameless" (Revelation 14:1, 5, NIV).

"These six things the LORD hates, Yes, seven are an abomination to Him: A proud look, A lying tongue, Hands that shed innocent blood, A heart that devises wicked plans, Feet that are swift in running to evil, A false witness who speaks lies, And one who sows discord among brethren" (Proverbs 6:16–19, NKJV).

"The LORD detests lying lips, but he delights in men who are truthful" (Proverbs 12:22, NIV).

"The tongue of the righteous is choice silver, but the heart of the wicked is of little value" (Proverbs 10:20, NIV).

ADDITIONAL SCRIPTURE AND PROMISES

Ps. 10:7	*Prov. 10:18, 19*	*Zech. 8:17*
Ps. 31:18	*Prov. 12:17–19*	*Matt. 12:34*
Ps. 34:12–14	*Prov. 15:4*	*Eph. 4:29*
Ps. 39:1	*Prov. 17:4, 20*	*Col. 3:9*
Ps. 52:2	*Prov. 18:6, 7, 21*	*James 1:26*
Ps. 63:11	*Prov. 21:6, 23*	*James 3:5–9*
Ps. 141:3	*Prov. 26:28*	*1 Pet. 3:10*
Prov. 4:24	*Jer. 9:5, 8*	*1 John 3:18*

MARITAL PROBLEMS

PRECIOUS HEAVENLY FATHER,

My marriage is falling apart, and there doesn't seem to be anything I can do to fix it. I'm not sure I even want to try. Somehow the love that I once had has been swallowed up with resentment and anger. Unless You help me keep the commitment I made before You to honor, love, and support until death, this marriage won't survive.

I've seen the fulfillment of Proverbs 10:12 in myself, for my hatred of the things my mate has done has truly stirred up a lot of strife. But You have said that love covers all sins. Please put Your love in my heart and let me see the person I married through Your eyes. I renew the covenant of Joshua 24:15 with You to choose this day to serve You and You alone. I am trusting You to help me cast away my pride and make things right. I know I'm not perfect, and I know I share the blame for the problems we face.

Please forgive me for all the selfish mistakes I have made. Help me to love with Your love. I really want this marriage to work, and I believe what You have said in Ecclesiastes 4:9 and 10 that "Two are better than one" (NKJV)! And I believe Your Words in Mark 10:27 that with You, all things are possible. I'm pleading with You, Jesus, to save my marriage. I pray all these things in Your precious name. AMEN.

Promises About Marital Problems

"Hatred stirs up strife, But love covers all sins"
(Proverbs 10:12, NKJV).

" 'Choose for yourselves this day whom you will serve, . . .
But as for me and my house, we will serve the LORD' "
(Joshua 24:15, NKJV).

"Two are better than one, Because they have a good reward for
their labor. For if they fall, one will lift up his companion.
But woe to him who is alone when he falls, For he has no one
to help him up" (Ecclesiastes 4:9, 10, NKJV).

"But Jesus looked at them and said, 'With men it is impossible,
but not with God; for with God all things are possible' "
(Mark 10:27, NKJV).

Additional Scripture and Promises

Gen. 2:18	Eccles. 9:9	Eph. 5:1, 2, 21–33
Gen. 24:67	Mal. 2:14–16	Col. 3:12–19
Ps. 128:3, 4	Matt. 19:3–8	1 Thess. 5:23
Prov. 1:29	Mark 10:12, 13	2 Tim. 2:26
Prov. 3:5, 6	1 Cor. 7:3–5, 10–16	Heb. 13:4
Prov. 5:15–18	1 Cor. 13:4–8, 11	1 Pet. 1:22
Prov. 10:12	1 Cor. 14:1	1 Pet. 3:1–11
Prov. 12:4	Eph. 4:31, 32	1 John 4:12

MARRIAGE

DEAR FATHER IN HEAVEN,

I'm overwhelmed with gratitude that You have given me my heart's desire in the special person You have chosen to be my marriage partner. How very blessed I am!

I pray for a special blessing on my marriage, and I invite You to make Your love increase and overflow in us, as You have promised in 1 Thessalonians 3:12. May our love be the perfect love described in 1 John 4:18, that drives out all fear. We live in such a wicked world, and I know that unless You are first in our lives, we cannot possibly have a happy marriage.

Remove all selfishness and jealousy. Help me to always put the needs of my spouse above my own as You have instructed me to do in Philippians 2:3 and 4. Oh Lord, shield us from any thoughts of infidelity, for in Ecclesiastes 3:14 You have made it very clear that whatever You do is forever. I want Your "forever" love in our marriage!

I pray that we will be united in our love for You and to each other. Please, Father, be the Head of our home and fill our lives with Your joy, as You have promised in John 16:24! AMEN.

Promises About Marriage

*"May the Lord make your love increase and overflow
for each other" (1 Thessalonians 3:12, NIV).*

*"There is no fear in love. But perfect love drives out fear"
(1 John 4:18, NIV).*

*"In humility consider others better than yourselves.
Each of you should look not only to your own interests,
but also to the interests of others"
(Philippians 2:3, 4, NIV).*

*"Whatever God does, It shall be forever.
Nothing can be added to it, And nothing taken from it"
(Ecclesiastes 3:14, NKJV).*

*" 'Ask, and you will receive, that your joy may be full' "
(John 16:24, NKJV).*

Additional Scripture and Promises

Ruth 1:16, 17	*Song of Sol. 8:6–10*	*1 Cor. 7:10–16*
Ps. 128:3, 4	*Mal. 2:14*	*1 Cor. 11:3, 8–12*
Prov. 4:7, 8	*Matt. 19:4–8*	*1 Cor. 13:4–8*
Prov. 10:12	*Luke 16:18*	*Eph. 5:21–33*
Prov. 14:1	*Luke 20:34*	*Col. 3:18–21*
Prov. 31:10–30	*Rom. 7:2*	*Heb. 13:4*
Song of Sol. 5:16	*1 Cor. 6:16*	*1 Pet. 3:1–7*
Song of Sol. 7:10	*1 Cor. 7:2–5*	*1 John 4:7, 12*

MERCY

DEAR MERCIFUL FATHER IN HEAVEN,

I want so very much to be like You and do what is right. I don't want to sin. But so often I feel like the apostle Paul said of himself in Romans 7:15—I end up doing what I don't want to do! When I think of myself in contrast to Your majesty and holiness, my righteousness is like the filthy rags mentioned in Isaiah 64:6. But James 5:11 reminds me that You are full of compassion and mercy. Thank You for the promise in Isaiah 55:6 and 7 that if I turn to You, You *will* have mercy on me and freely pardon.

Lord, I'm turning to You right now and pleading for mercy—even though I'm so undeserving. My prayer is the prayer in Psalm 51:1 and 2, "Have mercy upon me, O God, According to Your lovingkindness; According to the multitude of Your tender mercies, Blot out my transgressions. Wash me thoroughly from my iniquity, And cleanse me from my sin" (NKJV).

And I claim the promise in Psalm 103:17 that Your mercy is from everlasting to everlasting—it never ends! Thank You, Lord. Help me never to forget what You have done for me, and may I show that same Christlike mercy to others. AMEN.

Promises About Mercy

"For what I am doing, I do not understand.
For what I will to do, that I do not practice;
but what I hate, that I do" (Romans 7:15, NKJV).

"All of us have become like one who is unclean, and all our
righteous acts are like filthy rags; we all shrivel up like a leaf,
and like the wind our sins sweep us away" (Isaiah 64:6, NIV).

"The Lord is full of compassion and mercy" (James 5:11, NIV).

"Seek the LORD while he may be found; call on him while he is
near. Let the wicked forsake his way and the evil man his thoughts.
Let him turn to the LORD, and he will have mercy on him, and to
our God, for he will freely pardon" (Isaiah 55:6, 7, NIV).

"Have mercy upon me, O God, According to Your lovingkind-
ness; According to the multitude of Your tender mercies, Blot out
my transgressions" (Psalm 51:1, NKJV).

"But the mercy of the LORD is from everlasting to everlasting
upon them that fear him, and his righteousness unto children's
children" (Psalm 103:17, KJV).

Additional Scripture and Promises

Exod. 33:19	*Ps. 136*	*Titus 3:5*
Deut. 4:31	*Ps. 145:8, 9*	*Heb. 4:16*
2 Chron. 30:9	*Dan. 9:9*	*Heb. 8:12*
Neh. 9:17–19, 27–31	*Joel 2:13*	*Isa. 63:7*
Ps. 5:7	*Jonah 4:2*	*Isa. 48:9*
Ps. 6:9	*Micah 7:18*	*Isa. 38:17*
Ps. 117:2	*Luke 6:36*	*Jer. 3:12*
Ps. 123:2, 3	*Rom. 9:15–18*	*Lam. 3:22, 32, 33*

OBEDIENCE

Dear Father in Heaven,

I love You, Lord, with all my heart and soul. But I realize that the way to show my love is by obeying You—not just in words and actions, but in my thoughts as well. Lord, You've promised in Jeremiah 7:23 that if I obey, You will be my God; if I walk in Your ways, all will go well with me.

Luke 11:28 says that if I love Your law and am obedient to it, I will be blessed. Oh Father, You know my heart. I want to serve You with blind obedience, but I am weak. When I feel the enemy pressuring me to disobey, help me to remember that the power to resist comes from You. Give me the courage and strength to do what is right. I want Your will to be fulfilled in my life that I may receive Your blessing!

Your law is perfect! Let me follow Your instructions in Deuteronomy 4:2. Don't let me be guilty of adding or subtracting anything, for I want to do exactly what You ask me to do. Even though worldly things may tempt me, Lord, I pray that You will give me willpower to respect You and keep Your commandments, because as Ecclesiastes 12:13 says, this is the whole duty of man. Take my hand, Lord, and don't let go. May I always be obedient to You. Amen.

Promises About Obedience

" ' "Obey me, and I will be your God and you will be my people.
Walk in all the ways I command you, that it may go well
with you" ' " (Jeremiah 7:23, NIV).

"[Jesus] replied, 'Blessed . . . are those who hear the word
of God and obey it' " (Luke 11:28, NIV).

" 'You shall not add to the word which I command you,
nor take anything from it, that you may keep the commandments
of the LORD your God which I command you' "
(Deuteronomy 4:2, NKJV).

"Now all has been heard; here is the conclusion
of the matter: Fear God and keep his commandments,
for this is the whole duty of man"
(Ecclesiastes 12:13, NIV).

Additional Scripture and Promises

Gen. 22:18	Ps. 40:8	John 7:17
Deut. 4:30, 31	Ps. 106:3	John 8:51
Josh. 24:24	Ps. 119:33, 34	John 13:17
1 Sam. 15:22	Job 36:11	John 14:23
2 Chron. 31:21	Isa. 1:19	John 15:10
Ezra 7:23	Jer. 26:13	Rom. 2:13
Ps. 18:24	Matt. 7:21–25	Phil. 4:9
Ps. 25:10	Luke 11:28	Heb. 5:8, 9

PARENTING

DEAR LOVING FATHER,

Thank You so much for my precious children! I feel so blessed to be their parent! Psalm 127:3 reminds me that my children are Your gift and reward to me! What an awesome responsibility You've placed in my hands. At times I feel so inadequate. I love them so much, and I don't want to mess up their lives. That's why I claim Your promise in Jeremiah 29:11 that Your plans for me and my children are for good and not disaster.

You've commissioned me in Proverbs 22:6 to train these children in the way they should go, but many times I don't know what to do! You have told me in Ephesians 6:4 to discipline them tenderly and not provoke them to anger and resentment. And in Proverbs 3:27, You remind me to not withhold good when they deserve it. But sometimes I fail miserably! So, Lord, I ask for Your wisdom which You have promised me in James 1:5.

I love my children with all my heart, and I can't imagine not having them in my life! But You love them even more than I do! Precious Savior, *I dedicate my children to You!* Oh Lord, I want more than anything to declare as Joshua did in Joshua 24:15, " 'as for me and my house, we will serve the LORD' " (NKJV). Show me how. Guide me in the way I should go! *Do whatever is necessary to save them!* I pray that someday soon, when You come in those clouds of glory, all of my children will be in Your kingdom, without one lost! Thank You for hearing and answering my prayer! AMEN.

Promises About Parenting

"Behold, children are a gift of the Lord,
The fruit of the womb is a reward" (Psalm 127:3, NASB).

" 'For I know the plans that I have for you,' says the Lord. 'They
are plans for good and not for disaster,
to give you a future and a hope' "
(Jeremiah 29:11, NLT).

"Train up a child in the way he should go, And when he is old
he will not depart from it" (Proverbs 22:6, NKJV).

"Fathers, do no irritate and provoke your children to anger
[do not exasperate them to resentment], but rear them [tenderly]
in the training and discipline and the counsel and admonition
of the Lord" (Ephesians 6:4, AMP).

"Do not withhold good from those who deserve it"
(Proverbs 3:27, NLT).

" 'But as for me and my house, we will serve the Lord' "
(Joshua 24:15, NKJV).

Additional Scripture and Promises

Gen. 18:19	*Prov. 17:6*	*Matt. 18:4*
Deut. 6:6–9	*Prov. 20:7*	*Mark 9:37*
Deut. 11:19–21	*Prov. 22:15*	*Mark 10:14–16*
Ps. 8:1, 2	*Prov. 23:13, 14*	*Acts 2:38, 39*
Ps. 128:5, 6	*Prov. 29:15, 17*	*Eph. 6:1–4*
Prov. 10:1	*Isa. 54:13*	*Col. 3:20*
Prov. 3:11, 12	*Mal. 2:15*	*2 Tim. 3:15*
Prov. 13:24	*Matt. 10:42*	*3 John 1:4*

PATIENCE

Dear Lord,

I'm not the most patient person. In fact, I struggle daily wanting instant results and perfection! I want things done now and in my time! I know patience is the first characteristic of love that is mentioned in 1 Corinthians 13:4, and it's one of the fruits of the Spirit listed in Galatians 5:22, 23. But as important as the exercise of patience is, I still find myself getting frustrated and acting impulsively. So, Lord, teach me to be patient, even if it's a painful process.

You say in Psalm 37:4 that if I delight in You, You'll give me the desires of my heart. Thank You for that promise. I know that sometimes Your plans for me don't happen immediately, so help me to patiently wait upon You and Your perfect timing as You have instructed me to do in Psalm 27:14.

Father, make me ever mindful of the wisdom of doing Your will. Help me to remember it is always about You and not me! May I follow Your advice in Psalm 37:7, 9 to rest in You and wait patiently, for those who wait upon the Lord will inherit the earth! What a promise! Please mold me, bend me, and shape me into the patient person You want me to be! I surrender myself to You. Amen.

Promises About Patience

"Love is patient, love is kind. It does not envy,
it does not boast, it is not proud" (1 Corinthians 13:4, 5, NIV).

"But the fruit of the Spirit is love, joy, peace, patience,
kindness, goodness, faithfulness, gentleness and self-control"
(Galatians 5:22, 23 NIV).

"Delight yourself also in the Lord, And He shall give you
the desires of your heart" (Psalm 37:4, NKJV).

"Wait on the Lord; Be of good courage,
And He shall strengthen your heart;
Wait, I say, on the Lord!" (Psalm 27:14, NKJV).

"Rest in the Lord, and wait patiently for Him;
Do not fret because of him who prospers in his way,
Because of the man who brings wicked schemes to pass. . . .
For evildoers shall be cut off; But those who wait on the Lord,
They shall inherit the earth" (Psalm 37:7, 9, NKJV).

Additional Scripture and Promises

Ps. 40:1–3	Micah 7:7	1 Thess. 5:14
Prov. 14:29	Matt. 24:13	1 Tim. 1:16
Prov. 15:18	Rom. 5:3–5	Heb. 6:12
Prov. 16:32	Rom. 8:25	James 5:7–11
Prov. 19:11	Rom. 12:12	1 Pet. 2:20
Prov. 20:22	2 Cor. 6:4	2 Pet. 1:5, 6
Eccles. 7:8	Gal. 6:9	Rev. 3:10–12
Lam. 3:26	Col. 1:10, 11	Rev. 14:12

PEACE

Dear Lord,

My life is pretty chaotic right now. It's as if I'm being buffeted by the wind and waves on the troubled waters of Galilee. Mark 4:39 tells how You stood up in that sinking boat and rebuked the storm. Oh Lord, I need You to stand up and say, "Peace, be still," to the forces that are troubling me.

You tell me in 1 Corinthians 14:33 that You are the Author of peace, not confusion. I claim the promise in Isaiah 26:3 that You will keep me not just in peace, but in *perfect* peace, if I just keep my mind on You and trust in You.

I am trusting You, Lord, to bless me with Your peace as You say You'll do in Psalm 29:11. I love Your promise in Isaiah 32:17: "The work of righteousness will be peace, And the effect of righteousness, quietness and assurance forever" (NKJV). And I'm holding on to Your words in John 14:27: " 'Peace I leave with you, My peace I give to you; not as the world gives do I give to you. Let not your heart be troubled, neither let it be afraid' " (NKJV).

Already, I'm feeling the winds of strife dying down. Thank You for giving me the gift of Your *perfect* peace. Amen.

Promises About Peace

*"Then He arose and rebuked the wind, and said to the sea,
'Peace, be still!' And the wind ceased and there was a great calm"
(Mark 4:39, NKJV).*

*"For God is not the author of confusion but of peace"
(1 Corinthians 14:33, NKJV).*

*" 'You will keep him in perfect peace,
Whose mind is stayed on You,
Because he trusts in You' " (Isaiah 26:3, NKJV).*

*"The LORD will give strength to His people;
The LORD will bless His people with peace"
(Psalm 29:11, NKJV).*

*"The work of righteousness will be peace, And the
effect of righteousness, quietness and assurance forever"
(Isaiah 32:17, NKJV).*

*" 'Peace I leave with you, My peace I give to you;
not as the world gives do I give to you. Let not your
heart be troubled, neither let it be afraid' "
(John 14:27, NKJV).*

Additional Scripture and Promises

Lev. 26:6	Matt. 5:9	Phil. 4:6, 7
Ps. 4:8	Mark 9:50	Col. 1:19, 20
Ps. 122:6–9	John 16:33	Col. 3:15
Prov. 3:24	Rom. 5:1, 2	1 Thess. 5:13
Isa. 26:2–4, 12	Rom. 14:19	2 Thess. 3:16
Isa. 32:18	2 Cor. 13:11	Heb. 12:14
Isa. 55:12	Gal. 5:22	1 Pet. 3:10–12
Isa. 57:20, 21	Eph. 2:13–17	2 Pet. 1:2

PERSECUTION
for CHRIST'S SAKE

DEAR HEAVENLY FATHER,

My world seems to be crashing in all around me. The more I strive to be close to You, the harder the devil works to make me miserable. Everything is going wrong in my life. Oh, dear Lord, I am crying out to You as David did in Psalm 7:1: "Save me from all them that persecute me" (KJV). I claim Your promise in Psalm 18:48 that You *will* deliver me from my enemies and will lift me up above those who rise against me.

I long to have a oneness with You. And I ask for love in my heart for the people who are hurting me, for You have told me in Matthew 5:44 to love my enemies and bless them that curse me. So, Lord, bless my enemies! Give them the things You know I'd like. Saying this is one thing—but You're going to have to give me that heart transplant You promised in Ezekiel 36:26, if I am going to really mean it.

I am claiming Your promise in Jeremiah 1:19 that You will rescue me. So instead of being worried, may I allow You to fill my heart with gladness. I am holding on to Your promise in Matthew 5:10: " 'Blessed are those who are persecuted because of righteousness, for theirs is the kingdom of heaven' " (NIV).

You are such an awesome God. Thank You for reminding me of what a privilege it is to be persecuted for Your sake. I love You. AMEN.

Promises About Persecution

"Save me from all them that persecute me" (Psalm 7:1, KJV).

"He delivers me from my enemies.
You also lift me up above those who rise against me"
(Psalm 18:48, NKJV).

"But I say unto you, Love your enemies, bless them that curse
you, do good to them that hate you, and pray for them which
despitefully use you, and persecute you" (Matthew 5:44, KJV).

" 'I will give you a new heart and put a new spirit within you;
I will take the heart of stone out of your flesh and give you a
heart of flesh' " (Ezekiel 36:26, NKJV).

" 'They will fight against you but will not overcome you,
for I am with you and will rescue you,' declares the LORD"
(Jeremiah 1:19, NIV).

" 'Blessed are those who are persecuted because of righteousness,
for theirs is the kingdom of heaven' " (Matthew 5:10, NIV).

Additional Scripture and Promises

Ps. 83:3	Luke 21:12–18	2 Tim. 3:11, 12
Ps. 91:5	Luke 22:33	2 Tim. 4:16
Prov. 9:8	John 15:20	Heb. 13:6
Isa. 41:10	John 16:33	1 Pet. 2:23
Isa. 54:17	Rom. 8:31–39	1 Pet. 3:12–14
Zech. 9:16	Rom. 12:14	1 Pet. 4:16
Matt. 5:10–12	2 Cor. 1:4	1 John 3:13
Matt. 10:19, 28	2 Tim. 2:3	Rev. 2:10

PERSEVERANCE

DEAR LORD,

I believe You have put within my heart dreams and goals of what You would like me to do for You. But when I hit obstacles and challenges, it's sometimes hard for me to keep going. So, Lord, I need You to give me the spiritual energy necessary not to let anything distract me, but to keep looking ahead to the goal You have for my life, as Paul admonishes me to do in Philippians 3:14. I'm encouraged with the assurance in Hebrews 10:36 that if I persevere and do Your will, You will fulfill Your promises.

So first of all, I claim the promise in 1 Corinthians 15:58 that if I stand firm and let nothing move me, my work for You will not be in vain. In addition, You say in James 1:12 that because I love You and persevere under trial, You will give me a crown of life. Thank You for that promise. But Lord, I want more than just something for myself. I want my work for You to influence the lives of others. I want them to learn to love You.

That's why I'm claiming the promise in Galatians 6:9 that if I don't become weary of doing good or give up, that at the proper time I will reap a harvest for You. Thank You, Jesus. AMEN.

Promises About Perseverance

"I press on toward the goal to win the [supreme and heavenly]
prize to which God in Christ Jesus is calling us upward"
(Philippians 3:14, AMP).

"You need to persevere so that when you have done the will of God,
you will receive what he has promised" (Hebrews 10:36, NIV).

"Stand firm, Let nothing move you. Always give yourselves fully
to the work of the Lord, because you know that your labor in the
Lord is not in vain" (1 Corinthians 15:58, NIV).

"Blessed is the man who perseveres under trial, because when he
has stood the test, he will receive the crown of life that God has
promised to those who love him" (James 1:12, NIV).

"Let us not become weary in doing good, for at the proper time we
will reap a harvest if we do not give up" (Galatians 6:9, NIV).

Additional Scripture and Promises

2 Chron. 15:7	*2 Cor. 4:17*	*James 5:11*
Job 23:10	*Phil. 1:6*	*1 Pet. 1:6, 7*
Ps. 17:5	*Phil. 3:12–14*	*1 Pet. 5:8, 9*
Matt. 10:22	*1 Tim. 4:16*	*2 Pet. 2:20*
Luke 6:22, 23	*2 Tim. 2:11, 12*	*1 John 2:17*
Rom. 5:3, 4	*Heb. 10:23*	*Rev. 3:11*
Rom. 8:18	*Heb. 12:1–3*	*Rev. 21:6, 7*
Rom. 13:11	*James 1:2–5*	

PRAISE

Dear Loving Father in Heaven,
Creator of the Universe, Almighty God,

So many times I come to You asking for things or pleading for Your divine intervention and direction. But this time I ask for nothing. Today I approach Your throne room for no other reason but to praise Your holy name. For as Psalm 113:5–9 says, who is like the Lord our God? You dwell on high, and yet You humble Yourself. You raise the poor out of the dust and lift the needy out of the ash heap. You grant the barren woman a home.

Oh God, You are all powerful, merciful, exalted, and the Most High. You are my Protector, Deliverer, Provider, Maker, and Healer. You are my Rock, Shield, Fortress, Refuge, Comforter, Savior, and King. You are worthy to be praised, as David sang on the day You delivered him from Saul and his enemies (Psalm 18:3). I praise You for Your goodness and for Your wonderful works for me (Psalm 139:14). I praise You for what You have done for my soul by granting me mercy and by hearing and answering my prayers.

Lord, let me never forget how great You are. And as Psalm 34:1 says, may praises to You "continually be in my mouth" (NKJV). Amen.

PROMISES ABOUT PRAISE

"Who is like the LORD our God,
Who dwells on high, Who humbles Himself
to behold The things that are in the heavens and in the earth?
He raises the poor out of the dust, And lifts the needy
out of the ash heap, That He may seat him with princes—
With the princes of His people.
He grants the barren woman a home,
Like a joyful mother of children"
(Psalm 113:5–9, NKJV).

"I will call upon the LORD, who is worthy to be praised"
(Psalm 18:3, NKJV).

"I will praise You, for I am fearfully and wonderfully made;
Marvelous are Your works, And that my soul knows very well"
(Psalm 139:14, NKJV).

"I will bless the LORD at all times;
His praise shall continually be in my mouth"
(Psalm 34:1, NKJV).

ADDITIONAL SCRIPTURE AND PROMISES

Exod. 15:2	*Ps. 100*	*Matt. 5:16*
Ps. 42:4, 11	*Ps. 103:2, 3*	*John 9:24*
Ps. 47:1, 6, 7	*Ps. 107:2, 8, 21, 22, 31, 32*	*John 12:43*
Ps. 48:1, 10	*Ps. 149:1–6*	*Acts 2:46, 47*
Ps. 63:3–5	*Ps. 150*	*Acts 4:21*
Ps. 71:8, 14	*Isa. 12:4, 5*	*Rom. 2:29*
Ps. 86:12	*Isa. 63:7*	*Eph. 5:18–20*
Ps. 96:1–4, 8	*Joel 2:26*	*Rev. 7:12*

PRAYER

DEAR FATHER WHO ART IN HEAVEN,

I am humbled that You, the Creator and Master of the universe, have given me the privilege of talking with You in prayer—anytime, anywhere. It means so much to me to know I can tell You things that I can't share with anyone else, and that You'll understand and satisfy my longing soul, as it says You'll do in Psalm 107:9.

In fact, in Jeremiah 33:3, You make it clear that You want me to call on You so You can answer me and show me great and mighty things above and beyond what I can imagine. You have promised in Matthew 7:7 that if I ask, You'll answer; if I seek, I'll find; and if I knock, You'll open the door for me.

You have also promised in Matthew 21:22, that if I ask for something, *believing,* You'll give it to me. Lord, I'm absolutely awed by the reality that I'm not worthy to look upon Your glory, and yet You want to communicate with me so intimately that Your Word can live in me and You can give me the desires of my heart, as You say You will in John 15:7 and 8. I claim these promises.

Thank You, Jesus, for answered prayer. AMEN.

PROMISES ABOUT PRAYER

"For He satisfies the longing soul,
And fills the hungry soul with goodness"
(Psalm 107:9, NKJV).

"Call unto me, and I will answer thee, and shew thee
great and mighty things, which thou knowest not"
(Jeremiah 33:3, KJV).

"Ask, and it shall be given you; seek, and ye shall find;
knock, and it shall be opened unto you" (Matthew 7:7, KJV).

"And all things, whatsoever ye shall ask in prayer,
believing, ye shall receive" (Matthew 21:22, KJV).

" 'If you abide in Me, and My words abide in you, you will ask
what you desire, and it shall be done for you. By this My Father is
glorified, that you bear much fruit; so you will be My disciples' "
(John 15:7, 8, NKJV).

ADDITIONAL SCRIPTURE AND PROMISES

1 Chron. 7:14 *Matt. 5:44, 45* *Phil. 4:6, 7*
Ps. 34:4–6, 17 *Matt. 6:5–13* *Col. 1:9*
Ps. 50:15 *Matt. 7:7, 8, 11* *1 Tim. 2:1, 8*
Ps. 91:15 *Mark 11:24* *James 5:15, 16*
Ps. 145:18, 19 *Luke 11:9* *1 Pet. 3:12*
Isa. 65:24 *John 15:7* *1 Pet. 4:7*
Jer. 29:12–14 *Rom. 8:26, 27, 34* *1 John 5:14, 15*
Zech. 13:9 *Rom. 12:12*

PRIDE

Dear Precious Savior,

I long to have a closer walk with You and yet I know that is not possible as long as I hang on to my foolish pride. You have blessed me with so many talents. It's easy to get puffed up when people are telling me how good I am, or worse, when I actually feel my opinions and ways of doing things are superior! Keep me from thinking I'm better or more important than others. Proverbs 16:18 says that "Pride goes before destruction, And a haughty spirit before a fall" (NKJV). And Proverbs 26:12 says there is more hope for a fool than for a proud person! Oh Lord, do whatever is necessary to keep me from being a proud person! I don't want to be this way!

Pride is a horrible trait, for it was pride that turned Lucifer, the angel of light, into Satan, the demon of darkness. You make it very clear in Proverbs 21:4 that a proud heart is a sin and all sin will separate me from You! That is why I plead with You, my Father, to strip me of all selfishness. And may I always give You the praise, honor, and glory! I pray for humility!

Dear Lord Jesus, give me power through the Holy Spirit to resist the temptation of pride. In James 4:7 and 10, You have promised that if I submit myself to You, the devil will flee and that if I humble myself before You, You will lift me up. I claim these promises! I humbly submit my life totally to You and lay all pride at the Cross. Thank You, Jesus. Amen.

Promises About Pride

"*Pride goes before destruction,*
And a haughty spirit before a fall.
Better to be of a humble spirit with the lowly,
Than to divide the spoil with the proud"
(Proverbs 16:18, 19, NKJV).

"*Do you see a man wise in his own eyes?*
There is more hope for a fool than for him"
(Proverbs 26:12, NKJV).

"*A haughty look, a proud heart,*
And the plowing of the wicked are sin"
(Proverbs 21:4, NKJV).

" '*God opposes the proud but gives grace to the humble.*'
Submit yourselves, then, to God. Resist the devil,
and he will flee from you. . . . Humble yourselves before the
Lord, and he will lift you up" *(James 4:6, 7, 10, NIV).*

Additional Scripture and Promises

1 Sam. 2:3	Eccles. 4:13	Rom. 12:3, 16
Ps. 18:27	Isa. 13:11	2 Cor. 3:5
Ps. 36:2	Jer. 9:23, 24	2 Cor. 10:13, 17, 18
Ps. 40:4	Dan. 4:37	Phil. 2:3
Prov. 3:5	Matt. 18:2–4	2 Tim. 3:1–4
Prov. 6:16, 17	Matt. 23:11, 12	James 4:6
Prov. 15:25, 33	Luke 18:9–14	1 Pet. 5:5, 6
Prov. 28:11, 25, 26	John 8:50	1 John 2:15, 16

PROTECTION

Dear Lord,

I'm frightened because of all the evil in this world. I read of terrible things that have happened to others, and I fear for my safety. I know from John 10:10 that the devil is ready to steal, kill, and destroy—especially God's people. But Jesus, You came so that I might have an abundant life and not have to be afraid. Take away this fear in my heart. Fill me with the assurance of Your protection. Psalm 97:10 tells me that You guard the lives of Your faithful ones.

I worry about things I can't control—such as natural disasters that come so suddenly people can't escape. I pray that You'll keep my home and my family safe, as You have said You would do in Psalm 91:9–11: "If you make the Most High your dwelling . . . then no harm will befall you, no disaster will come near your tent. For he will command his angels concerning you to guard you in all your ways" (NIV).

Thank You for the promise in Psalm 32:7, that You'll hide me and protect me from trouble. And for the assurance of Psalm 121:7, 8: "The Lord will keep you from all harm—he will watch over your life; the Lord will watch over your coming and going both now and forevermore" (NIV).

I praise You for Your watch care over me, for Your guardian angels, and for Your promises of protection. Amen.

Promises About Protection

" 'The thief does not come except to steal, and to kill, and to destroy. I have come that they may have life, and that they may have it more abundantly' " (John 10:10, NKJV).

"The Lord . . . guards the lives of his faithful ones" (Psalm 97:10, NIV).

"If you make the Most High your dwelling—even the Lord, who is my refuge—then no harm will befall you, no disaster will come near your tent. For he will command his angels concerning you to guard you in all your ways" (Psalm 91:9–11, NIV).

"You are my hiding place; You shall preserve me from trouble" (Psalm 32:7, NKJV).

"The Lord will keep you from all harm— he will watch over your life; the Lord will watch over your coming and going both now and forevermore" (Psalm 121:7, 8, NIV).

Additional Scripture and Promises

Deut. 33:12, 27	Ps. 112:7	Prov. 18:10
Ps. 4:8	Ps. 121	Isa. 25:4
Ps. 27:1, 5	Ps. 145:20	Isa. 43:1, 2
Ps. 32:7	Prov. 1:32, 33	Isa. 54:17
Ps. 34:7, 17	Prov. 2:7, 8	Ezek. 34:28
Ps. 40:11	Prov. 3:24	Matt. 7:24, 25
Ps. 41:1, 2	Prov. 10:29	2 Thess. 3:3
Ps. 91:4–16	Prov. 11:8	1 Pet. 3:13

PURITY

Dear Heavenly Father,

I'm ashamed at how I keep allowing things of this world and my selfish desires to crowd out Your pure love. Isaiah 33:15 and 16 says I should walk righteously, speak uprightly, stop my ears from hearing violence, and shut my eyes from seeing evil. Oh Lord, I am unclean—and I so much desire to be pure. My soul cries out to You as David did in Psalm 51:10: "Create in me a clean heart, O God, And renew a steadfast spirit within me" (NKJV).

Help me stand by the conviction found in Psalm 101:3: "I will set nothing wicked before my eyes" (NKJV). But without You living in my heart, there is no hope. So, thank You for reminding me in Psalm 119:11 to hide Your Word in my heart that I might not sin against You!

I long to see You face to face and live eternally with You as Matthew 5:8 promises for those who have a pure heart. First John 1:7 tells me that if I walk in the light as You are in the light, the blood of Jesus Christ will cleanse me from all my sin.

Oh, precious Savior, take my hand and guide me in a life of purity that I may always abide with You. Because of Your love for me, I claim all that You have promised, in Jesus' name. Amen.

Promises About Purity

"He who walks righteously and speaks uprightly, He who despises the gain of oppressions, Who gestures with his hands, refusing bribes, Who stops his ears from hearing of bloodshed, And shuts his eyes from seeing evil: He will dwell on high; His place of defense will be the fortress of rocks; Bread will be given him, His water will be sure" (Isaiah 33:15, 16, NKJV).

"Create in me a clean heart, O God, And renew a steadfast spirit within me" (Psalm 51:10, NKJV).

"I will set nothing wicked before my eyes" (Psalm 101:3, NKJV).

"How can a young man keep his way pure? By living according to your word. . . . I have hidden your word in my heart that I might not sin against you" (Psalm 119:9, 11, NIV).

"Blessed are the pure in heart: for they shall see God" (Matthew 5:8, KJV).

"But if we walk in the light as He is in the light, we have fellowship with one another, and the blood of Jesus Christ His Son cleanses us from all sin" (1 John 1:7, NKJV).

Additional Scripture and Promises

2 Sam. 22:27	Ps. 101:3	Mark 7:21–23
Job 8:6	Ps. 119:9, 11	Rom. 12:1, 2
Job 11:4	Prov. 15:26	Phil. 4:8
Job 16:17	Prov. 20:11	1 Tim. 1:5
Job 31:1	Prov. 21:8	Titus 1:15
Ps. 12:6	Prov. 22:11	James 3:17
Ps. 19:8	Isa. 33:15, 16	1 Pet. 1:13–15
Ps. 24:3, 4	Matt. 5:8	1 John 1:7

REPENTANCE

MY PRECIOUS REDEEMER,

I come to You as a sinner not even worthy to approach Your throne room. I'm so sorry for hurting You. My heart aches to be free from sinning against You. Oh Lord, please give me a hatred for sin! You are a perfect God of truth and without iniquity. You are so holy I can't look upon Your face, and yet, Psalm 103:3 says You will forgive all my iniquities.

You have told me in Luke 5:32 that the very reason You came to this earth was to call sinners like me to repentance. You have made it very clear in 1 John 1:9 that if I confess my sins, You will forgive and cleanse me. I cling to Your promise in 2 Peter 3:9 that You are longsuffering toward us, not willing that any should perish but that all should come to repentance. Lord, I am so sorry for sinning against You. Please forgive me! Take away my sins. Bury them as deep as the deepest sea.

Thank You for promising in Isaiah 43:25 to not only blot out my sins, but to forget them! I believe that because You died for me and I have accepted You as my Savior, I have salvation—even though I don't deserve it. Thank You for paying the price for my sins and giving me Your abundant life. Your grace is amazing! In Jesus' name I praise and rejoice in You. AMEN.

PROMISES ABOUT REPENTANCE

"Bless the LORD, O my soul; And forget not all His benefits: Who forgives all your iniquities" (Psalm 103:2, 3, NKJV).

" 'I have not come to call the righteous, but sinners, to repentance' " (Luke 5:32, NKJV).

"If we confess our sins, He is faithful and just to forgive us our sins and to cleanse us from all unrighteousness" (1 John 1:9, NKJV).

"The Lord is not slack concerning His promise, as some count slackness, but is longsuffering toward us, not willing that any should perish but that all should come to repentance" (2 Peter 3:9, NKJV).

" 'I, even I, am He who blots out your transgressions for My own sake; And I will not remember your sins' " (Isaiah 43:25, NKJV).

ADDITIONAL SCRIPTURE AND PROMISES

RESPECT

DEAR FATHER IN HEAVEN,

I'm living in a world where people blatantly show contempt and disrespect for others. I admit that sometimes it's hard for me to treat others with respect when they say hurtful things to me. And yet, I know You don't want me to even think evil thoughts! I even hear people take Your name in vain. Oh how this must hurt You! But Romans 2:11 says You don't show favoritism—nor do You treat them disrespectfully.

You have given us the standard when You say in Matthew 7:12 that we should treat others as we would like to be treated. You tell us in Romans 12:10 to love with genuine affection and to take delight in honoring each other. Ephesians 4:32 says we should be imitators of You—kind, compassionate, and forgiving. Titus 3:1 and 2 adds to this list: peaceable, considerate, and showing true humility. And 1 Peter 3:8 and 9 emphasizes being tenderhearted and courteous, "not returning evil for evil or reviling for reviling" (NKJV), but rather blessing each other that we may inherit a blessing. I claim that promise, Lord.

Help me to treat people with honor, esteem, and respect, no matter how they treat me. And in doing so, may I reap the reward of Your blessing. More importantly, help me to always give You respect, honor, praise, and glory. This is my prayer in Jesus' name. AMEN.

Promises About Respect

"For God does not show favoritism" (Romans 2:11, NIV).

" 'Therefore, whatever you want men to do to you, do also to them' " (Matthew 7:12, NKJV).

"Don't just pretend that you love others. Really love them. . . . Love each other with genuine affection, and take delight in honoring each other" (Romans 12:9, 10, NLT).

"Be kind and compassionate to one another, forgiving each other, just as in Christ God forgave you" (Ephesians 4:32, NIV).

"Remind the people to be subject to rulers and authorities, to be obedient, to be ready to do whatever is good, to slander no one, to be peaceable and considerate, and to show true humility toward all men" (Titus 3:1, 2, NIV).

"Finally, all of you be of one mind, having compassion for one another; love as brothers, be tenderhearted, be courteous; not returning evil for evil" (1 Peter 3:8, 9, NKJV).

Additional Scripture and Promises

Lev. 19:15, 32	Luke 18:9–14	Col. 1:3
Deut. 10:17	Acts 10:34–36	Col. 3:11–14, 24, 25
Ps. 138:6	Rom. 12:9, 16	Col. 4:1
Prov. 19:6	1 Cor. 13:4, 5	1 Tim. 5:21
Prov. 28:21	1 Cor. 15:33	Heb. 10:24
Prov. 31:30	Eph. 5:21–26, 33	James 2:9
Matt. 5:45–47	Phil. 2:4	1 Pet. 5:5, 6
Luke 6:35, 36	Gal. 3:26–28	

REST

DEAR FATHER IN HEAVEN,

It feels so good to just stop for a moment and whisper a prayer to You. You are like an oasis in the middle of the hustle and bustle of my life—with too much to do and not enough time to do it. I have so many things vying for my attention; I don't even know where to start. And at the end of the day, after rushing around trying to get everything done, it seems as if I have accomplished so little.

Sometimes it feels like one day just blurs into the next. So, thank You, Lord, for reminding me in Matthew 11:28–30 to come to You for rest and You will make my burden lighter. You are the only One who really understands how much is expected of me. I'm claiming Your promise in Jeremiah 31:25 that You will refresh the weary and satisfy the faint. I rejoice as David did in Psalm 62:1 and 2, for in You I have found a special kind of rest that truly refreshes my soul.

I treasure our quiet time together so much. Lord, please keep me close to You and shelter me from unnecessary tasks. Let me find the rest I so desperately seek that You have promised in Psalm 91:1. Thank You for hearing and answering my prayer. I love You and ask everything in the holy name of Jesus who died to save me. Amen.

Promises About Rest

" 'Come to me, all you who are weary and burdened,
and I will give you rest. Take my yoke upon you and learn from
me, for I am gentle and humble in heart, and you will find rest
for your souls. For my yoke is easy and my burden is light' "
(Matthew 11:28–30, NIV).

" 'I will refresh the weary and satisfy the faint' "
(Jeremiah 31:25, NIV).

"My soul finds rest in God alone; my salvation comes from him.
He alone is my rock and my salvation; he is my fortress,
I will never be shaken" (Psalm 62:1, 2, NIV).

"He who dwells in the shelter of the Most High will
rest in the shadow of the Almighty"
(Psalm 91:1, NIV).

Additional Scripture and Promises

Exod. 33:14	Ps. 121	Rom. 5:1, 2
Ps. 4:8	Prov. 29:25	Rom. 8:28
Ps. 23:1–3	Isa. 7:4	Rom. 14:19
Ps. 37:5–7	Isa. 28:12	1 Cor. 14:33
Ps. 55:22	Isa. 32:17, 18	Phil. 4:8, 11–13, 19
Ps. 91	Jer. 6:16	Heb. 4:9–11
Ps. 116:1–8	Matt. 6:33, 34	James 4:7

SABBATH

DEAR FATHER WHO ART IN HEAVEN,

I come to You asking for the strength and willpower to keep Your Sabbath day holy. I know how important it is to You because You wrote the commandment not once, but twice with Your own finger on a tablet of stone: " 'Remember the Sabbath day, to keep it holy' " (NKJV). I have read that text over and over again in Exodus 20:8–11 just trying to digest it all. You make it very clear that I am not to do any work on the seventh-day Sabbath.

You didn't say "Worship Me on any day you choose." You said the seventh day! Sometimes I'm tempted to sleep in on Sabbath, skipping church since I worked hard all week. Or if my boss calls and tells me they really need me at work, I find myself rationalizing that it really doesn't matter, as long as I don't do it all the time. But then I read Your counsel in Jeremiah 17:21 and 22 to " ' " 'bear no burden on the Sabbath day, . . . nor do any work, but hallow the Sabbath day, as I have commanded your fathers' " ' " (NKJV).

Oh Lord, forgive me! Help me show my love for You by keeping Your commandments as You have asked me to do in John 14:15. And I claim Your promise in Isaiah 58:13 and 14 that if I refrain from doing my own pleasure on Your holy day, and call the Sabbath a delight, You will cause me to ride on the high hills of the earth. Precious Savior, You have done so much for me. It is a privilege to honor, praise, and worship You on Your holy Sabbath. I love You, Father. AMEN.

Promises About Sabbath

" 'Remember the Sabbath day, to keep it holy. Six days you shall labor and do all your work, but the seventh day is the Sabbath of the Lord your God. In it you shall do no work: you, nor your son, nor your daughter, nor your manservant, nor your maidservant, nor your cattle, nor your stranger who is within your gates. For in six days the Lord made the heavens and the earth, the sea, and all that is in them, and rested the seventh day. Therefore the Lord blessed the Sabbath day and hallowed it' " (Exodus 20:8–11, NKJV).

" ' "Thus says the Lord: 'Take heed to yourselves, and bear no burden on the Sabbath day, nor bring it in by the gates of Jerusalem; nor carry a burden out of your houses on the Sabbath day, nor do any work, but hallow the Sabbath day, as I commanded your fathers' " ' " (Jeremiah 17:21, 22, NKJV).

" 'If you love Me, keep My commandments' " (John 14:15, NKJV).

" 'If you turn away your foot from the Sabbath, From doing your pleasure on My holy day, And call the Sabbath a delight, The holy day of the Lord honorable, And shall honor Him, not doing your own ways, Nor finding your own pleasure, Nor speaking your own words, Then you shall delight yourself in the Lord; And I will cause you to ride on the high hills of the earth, And feed you with the heritage of Jacob your father. The mouth of the Lord has spoken' " (Isaiah 58:13, 14, NKJV).

Additional Scripture and Promises

Gen. 2:2, 3	Isa. 56:2, 6, 7	Mark 15:42
Exod. 16:4, 23, 29, 30	Isa. 66:23	Mark 16:1
Exod. 23:12	Jer. 17:21–27	Luke 23:54–56
Exod. 31:15–17	Ezek. 20:12, 13, 20	Rev. 1:10
Exod. 35:2	Matt. 12:1, 2, 8–12	Rev. 12:17
Lev. 23:3	Matt. 24:20, 21	Rev. 14:12
Deut. 5:12–15	Mark 2:27, 28	Rev. 22:14
Neh. 13:15–22	Mark 6:2	

SALVATION

Precious Savior,

How can I ever thank You enough for giving me a new life in You? Your Word is my comfort and my joy. I embrace Your gift of salvation. I like to personalize Your words in John 3:16 this way: "For God so loved me that He gave His only begotten Son, that if I believe in Him I will not perish but have everlasting life." I deserve to pay the price for my own sins, but I lay hold of Your promise in 1 Thessalonians 5:9 that You did not appoint me to suffer wrath but to receive salvation through my Lord Jesus Christ.

Thank You, too, for Your promise in John 11:25 and 26, assuring me that You are the Resurrection and the Life and that whoever lives and believes in You, shall never die. Thank You for Your gift on Calvary that I may have eternal life! You revealed Your true mission on earth in Luke 19:10—to seek and save the lost. I was lost, but now I'm saved! And in John 6:40, You reassure me that " 'everyone who sees the Son and believes in Him may have everlasting life' " (NKJV). I embrace You, my Lord and my Redeemer. Thank You for Your saving grace.

You are so filled with love for me that my only response is to love You more and more each day, as I eagerly wait for You to come back and take me home with You for eternity! Amen.

Promises About Salvation

" 'For God so loved the world that He gave His only begotten Son, that whoever believes in Him should not perish but have everlasting life' " (John 3:16, NKJV).

"For God did not appoint us to suffer wrath but to receive salvation through our Lord Jesus Christ" (1 Thessalonians 5:9, NIV).

"Jesus said to her, 'I am the resurrection and the life. He who believes in Me, though he may die, he shall live. And whoever lives and believes in Me shall never die. Do you believe this?' " (John 11:25, 26, NKJV).

" 'For the Son of Man came to seek and to save what was lost' " (Luke 19:10, NIV).

" 'And this is the will of Him who sent Me, that everyone who sees the Son and believes in Him may have everlasting life; and I will raise him up at the last day' " (John 6:40, NKJV).

Additional Scripture and Promises

Ps. 3:8	Prov. 28:18	2 Tim. 1:9
Ps. 20:6	Isa. 35:4	Heb. 7:25
Ps. 34:18, 22	Isa. 59:1	1 Pet. 1:3–9
Ps. 37:39	Luke 1:77, 78	2 Pet. 3:9
Ps. 40:2	Rom. 6:23	1 John 3:1, 2
Ps. 62:1, 2	Rom. 10:9–11, 13	Rev. 21:3, 4, 7
Ps. 85:9	Gal. 1:4	Rev. 22:14–17
Prov. 20:22	1 Tim. 2:3, 4	

SALVATION
of CHILDREN

DEAR FATHER IN HEAVEN,

I'm pleading with You to save my children! I want them to know and love You as I do. My heart is heavy, watching them make choices that are leading them further and further away from You. The values, pleasures, and sinful things of this world appear so enticing. As 1 Peter 5:8 says, the devil is running around like a lion, seeking whom he may devour. I hear him roaring at my door, wanting to destroy my children. Oh Lord, You said in Isaiah 49:25 that You will contend with him who contends with me—and save my children. I take You at Your Word.

Please place a hedge of protection around them as You promised to do in Hosea 2:6, so they will resist the temptation to experiment with anything that will dull their conscience and destroy their desire to be closer to You. And one more thing, Lord, please don't let the mistakes I made with my children keep them from a saving relationship with You. Don't let their rebellion against me cause them to rebel against You. Instead, I pray that You will knit our hearts together in love as You have said You would do in Malachi 4:6, so they can see Your love more clearly.

Oh Lord, I plead with You for the salvation of my children. Thank You for loving them even more than I do.
AMEN.

Promises About the Salvation of Children

*"Be sober, be vigilant; because your adversary the devil
walks about like a roaring lion, seeking whom he may devour"*
(1 Peter 5:8, NKJV).

*"But the LORD says, . . . 'For I will fight those
who fight you, and I will save your children'"*
(Isaiah 49:25, NLT).

*"'Therefore, behold, I will hedge up your way with thorns,
And wall her in, So that she cannot find her paths'"*
(Hosea 2:6, NKJV).

*"'And he will turn The hearts of the fathers to the children,
And the hearts of the children to their fathers,
Lest I come and strike the earth with a curse'"*
(Malachi 4:6, NKJV).

Additional Scripture and Promises

Deut. 11:18–21	*Isa. 44:3*	*Acts 16:31*
Ps. 102:24–28	*Isa. 54:13*	*Eph. 6:4*
Ps. 127	*Jer. 31:16, 17*	*2 Tim. 3:15*
Prov. 17:6	*Mark 10:14–16*	
Prov. 22:6	*Acts 2:38, 39*	

SALVATION
of SINNERS

DEAR FATHER IN HEAVEN,

My heart is breaking over those who are lost. And what's so sad is that many don't even realize their spiritual condition! They're like the prodigal son—they are so busy enjoying the things of the world they don't hear the Father's pleas to come home. They don't realize that it won't be long until the money runs out, and the worldly pleasures grow meaningless, and they will find themselves stuck in a "pigpen" far from home.

I know, precious Lord, Your heart is breaking too—for these are Your children. Luke 19:10 says that You came " 'to seek and to save what was lost' " (NIV). If only they knew that the greatest peace and pleasure in the whole world is found in a saving relationship with You. Oh Lord, I claim these "children" for Your kingdom. My earnest desire is to spend eternity with them. I know Isaiah 59:1 says that Your "hand is not shortened, That it cannot save; Nor [Your] ear heavy, That it cannot hear" (NKJV).

I claim the promise of Jeremiah 31:17: " 'So there is hope for your future,' declares the LORD. 'Your children will return to their own land' " (NIV). Thank You for Your promise in Hosea 14:4: " 'I will heal their backsliding, I will love them freely' " (NKJV). Oh loving Father, I plead with You for the salvation of the lost. In Jesus' name who died to save them. AMEN.

PROMISES ABOUT THE SALVATION OF SINNERS

" 'For the Son of Man came to seek
and to save what was lost' "
(Luke 19:10, NIV).

"Behold, the LORD's hand is not shortened,
That it cannot save; Nor His ear heavy,
That it cannot hear"
(Isaiah 59:1, NKJV).

" 'So there is hope for your future,'
declares the LORD. 'Your children
will return to their own land' "
(Jeremiah 31:17, NIV).

" 'I will heal their backsliding,
I will love them freely' "
(Hosea 14:4, NKJV).

ADDITIONAL SCRIPTURE AND PROMISES

Deut. 20:4	Ps. 62:1, 2	Rom. 1:16
Job 22:29	Isa. 61:10	Rom. 10:9–13
Ps. 3:8	Matt. 1:21	Eph. 2:8, 9
Ps. 7:10	Mark 10:26, 27	1 Tim. 1:15
Ps. 20:6	John 3:16, 17	2 Tim. 1:9
Ps. 34:22	Acts 2:47	Titus 3:3–5
Ps. 37:39	Acts 4:12	Heb. 7:25
Ps. 40:2	Acts 16:30, 31	1 Pet. 1:3–9

SECURITY

DEAR HEAVENLY FATHER,

Everyday the news is flooded with reports of terrible things happening to innocent people. With the devil walking around like a roaring lion seeking whom he can devour (1 Peter 5:8), I realize there is no safety in this world—except in You. So, Lord, protect me today and hold me close to You. I know You love me, and I can't imagine any place more secure than being held in Your arms.

In Psalm 91:4, You've promised that I can take refuge under Your wings and that You'll cover me with Your feathers. Proverbs 18:10 assures me that Your name alone is a strong tower that I can run to and be safe. Help me, Lord, to cling to Your promise in Psalm 121:7 and 8 that You'll preserve me wherever I go so I can dwell in safety. Take away all my fears! Especially at night, Lord, let my insecurity go away as I repeat Your promise in Psalm 4:8, "I will both lie down in peace, and sleep; For You alone, O LORD, make me dwell in safety" (NKJV).

I am claiming Your promise in Proverbs 1:33 that if I listen to You, I will be secure, without fear of evil! Wow! What an incredible affirmation of Your love for me! Precious Savior, I am listening and I choose to put my faith and trust in You. AMEN.

Promises About Security

*"Be sober, be vigilant; because your adversary the devil walks
about like a roaring lion, seeking whom he may devour"
(1 Peter 5:8, NKJV).*

*"He shall cover you with His feathers,
And under His wings you shall take refuge;
His truth shall be your shield and buckler"
(Psalm 91:4, NKJV).*

*"The name of the LORD is a strong tower;
The righteous run to it and are safe"
(Proverbs 18:10, NKJV).*

*"The LORD shall preserve you from all evil; He shall preserve
your soul. The LORD shall preserve your going out and your
coming in From this time forth, and even forevermore"
(Psalm 121:7, 8, NKJV).*

*"I will both lie down in peace, and sleep; For You alone,
O LORD, make me dwell in safety" (Psalm 4:8, NKJV).*

*" 'But whoever listens to me will dwell safely,
And will be secure, without fear of evil' " (Proverbs 1:33, NKJV).*

Additional Scripture and Promises

Gen. 28:15	*Ps. 34:7, 17*	*John 10:27–29*
Job 11:13–20	*Ps. 46:1, 2*	*Rom. 8:31, 32, 38, 39*
Ps. 3:5, 6	*Ps. 112:7*	*2 Thess. 3:3*
Ps. 9:10	*Ps. 125:1*	*2 Tim. 1:7*
Ps. 16:5–9	*Prov. 16:20*	*Heb. 6:11, 12, 18–20*
Ps. 23:6	*Isa. 40:26*	*Heb. 13:6*
Ps. 27:1	*Isa. 41:10, 13*	*1 Pet. 1:3–5*
Ps. 32:7	*Isa. 43:2, 3*	*Jude 24, 25*

SELF-CONTROL

DEAR FATHER IN HEAVEN,

More than anything I want to spend eternity with You, but I know that unless I have more control of my actions, I won't be there. Self-control is something that I have always struggled with. It's hard to deny myself the things that I want, even when I know they're not good for me. I don't know why I'm out of control! I know in my heart Your coming is soon, and I want to heed Your counsel in 1 Peter 1:13 to prepare my mind for action, and to be self-controlled so that I can set my hope fully on the grace to be given me when Jesus comes!

In 1 Peter 4:7, You tell me once again how important it is to be clear-minded and self-controlled so that I can pray. Oh Jesus, give me victory that I may possess the self-discipline that I need to be close to You. Controlling my actions is so important to You that You mention it many times in Your holy Word; You've even made it one of the fruits of the Spirit listed in Galatians 5:22 and 23. Precious Father, reveal to me Your plan for my life and give me the strength to resist temptation.

May I put myself last and others first. I don't want to live according to my sinful nature as Paul warns against in Romans 8:13. I want to live a pure clean life, always making good choices. Thank You, Lord, for being such a good example of self-denial. I want to be more like You. AMEN.

Promises About Self-control

"Therefore, prepare your minds for action;
be self-controlled; set your hope fully on the grace
to be given you when Jesus Christ is revealed"
(1 Peter 1:13, NIV).

"The end of all things is near. Therefore be clear minded
and self-controlled so that you can pray"
(1 Peter 4:7, NIV).

"But the fruit of the Spirit is love, joy, peace, patience,
kindness, goodness, faithfulness, gentleness and self-control.
Against such there is no law"
(Galatians 5:22, 23, NIV).

"For if you live according to the sinful nature,
you will die; but if by the Spirit you put to death
the misdeeds of the body, you will live"
(Romans 8:13, NIV).

Additional Scripture and Promises

Deut. 4:9	Eccles. 2:11	Rom. 13:13, 14
Num. 15:39, 40	Isa. 26:3	1 Cor. 11:28
1 Sam. 15:23	Matt. 16:24	2 Cor. 3:5
Job 9:20	Matt. 26:41	2 Cor. 7:1
Prov. 3:5	John 5:30	Gal. 2:20
Prov. 12:15	John 15:5	Titus 2:11–13
Prov. 25:28	Rom. 6:6–11	Heb. 2:18
Prov. 27:2	Rom. 12:1–3, 10	1 Pet. 5:8, 9

SELF-WORTH

Dear Father in Heaven,

Right now I'm not feeling very good about myself. Others seem to have more money, talent, friends, personality, and blessings. I know 2 Corinthians 10:12 warns that it's unwise to compare myself with others. So, Lord, when I'm tempted to let my mind dwell on Satan's lie about how worthless I am, please keep me focused on my true value because of what You see in me and Your sacrifice for me.

In Psalm 139:14, You make it very clear that I'm "fearfully and wonderfully made" (NKJV)! And in Psalm 139:17, You tell me that You are constantly thinking precious thoughts about me. But the best news is in John 3:16 that assures me that You love me, have redeemed me, and will give me eternal life because I believe in You. Wow! That is incredible! When I am tempted to feel bad about myself, may I always remember that You love me so much that You gave Your life to save me. Help me to realize just how truly valuable I am!

I claim Your promise of eternal life. Keep my mind stayed on You, instead of others. Forgive me for entertaining negative thoughts about myself—who You created! And thank You for loving me supremely. Amen.

PROMISES ABOUT SELF-WORTH

"But they, measuring themselves by themselves,
and comparing themselves among themselves,
are not wise" (2 Corinthians 10:12, NKJV).

"I will praise You, for I am fearfully and wonderfully made;
Marvelous are Your works" (Psalm 139:14, NKJV).

"How precious also are Your thoughts to me, O God!
How great is the sum of them!" (Psalm 139:17, NKJV).

" 'For God so loved the world that He gave
His only begotten Son, that whoever believes in Him
should not perish but have everlasting life' "
(John 3:16, NKJV).

ADDITIONAL SCRIPTURE AND PROMISES

SERVICE

Dear Almighty God,

You have done so much for me, and yet it seems I'm always asking for more—whether it's to find something, complete a project, get me out of trouble, or strengthen a weak character trait. I'll admit, the bulk of my prayers are pretty much about me! But as I read Matthew 25:32–40 about how You will separate the sheep from the goats at Your coming, I understand more fully Your explanation of who will inherit the kingdom. You make it so clear that it is those who feed the hungry, give water to the thirsty, show hospitality to strangers, nurse the sick, and show love to others.

Oh Lord, You came to serve others, and I want to follow Your example! Acts 10:38 says You went about constantly doing good, and 1 Corinthians 3:9 says that we are to be laborers with You. Lord, change my heart so that I will unselfishly meet the needs of others as You did. May I serve others wholeheartedly as Ephesians 6:7 and 8 tells me to—as if I were serving You, not men. And in doing so, may others see Your love shining through me.

Father, I want to be a "sheep," with my only motive that of being Your hands and Your feet here in this world. Give me the ability through the Holy Spirit to see who needs Your love today—and give me the strength and courage to carry out Your will. Thank You for using me in Your service. In Jesus' name. Amen.

Promises About Service

" 'Then the King will say to those on His right hand, "Come,
you blessed of My Father, inherit the kingdom prepared for you
from the foundation of the world: for I was hungry and you gave
Me food; I was thirsty and you gave Me drink; I was a stranger
and you took Me in; I was naked and you clothed Me; I was sick
and you visited Me; I was in prison and you came to Me" ' "
(Matthew 25:34–36, NKJV).

" 'Jesus . . . went about doing good . . .
for God was with Him' " (Acts 10:38, NKJV).

"We are labourers together with God"
(1 Corinthians 3:9, KJV).

"Serve wholeheartedly, as if you were serving the Lord,
not men, because you know that the Lord will reward everyone
for whatever good he does, whether he is slave or free"
(Ephesians 6:7, 8, NIV).

Additional Scripture and Promises

Josh. 24:15	Luke 14:27–30, 33	Rom. 12:1
1 Sam. 7:3	Luke 16:10–13	1 Cor. 9:19–23
1 Sam. 12:24	Luke 17:9, 10	2 Cor. 4:5–11
1 Chron. 28:9	John 3:27	Gal. 5:13
1 Chron. 29:5	John 12:26	Gal. 6:4–6, 9
Matt. 4:10	John 13:35	Col. 3:23–25
Luke 3:10–14	John 15:4, 5, 16, 17	James 1:22
Luke 10:33, 34, 38–42	John 16:2	

SEXUAL SINS

DEAR FATHER IN HEAVEN,

I fall on my face in shame before You for I am not worthy to even say Your name. My sins are more than I can count. I hate what I do, but I love my sin. Oh Lord, please give me a hatred for my sins. You have told me in 1 Corinthians 6:13 that "The body is not meant for sexual immorality, but for the Lord, and the Lord for the body" (NIV). I know I have not kept my body pure for You. My sin is so disgusting that I don't know how You or anyone else could love me. I want to stop, but I can't seem to help myself.

I read in 2 Peter 3:9 Your precious words of hope, for You have said that your are not slack concerning Your promise, as some count slackness, but You are longsuffering toward me, not willing that I should perish but that I should come to repentance. Lord, with all my heart I repent of my sins and lay hold of this promise. I am sustained by Your promise in 1 Corinthians 10:13 that You are faithful and that You will make a way of escape from my temptations!

I believe You have the power to deliver me. In fact, in Psalm 56:13 it says that You have already "delivered my soul from death," and "delivered my feet from falling" (NKJV). I know this is true because of Jesus' sacrifice on the cross. I claim the blood of Jesus Christ that was shed for me on Calvary. I ask all this in Jesus' precious name who died to save me. AMEN.

Promises About Sexual Sins

" 'Food for the stomach and the stomach for food'—but God will destroy them both. The body is not meant for sexual immorality, but for the Lord, and the Lord for the body"
(1 Corinthians 6:13 NIV).

"The Lord is not slack concerning His promise, as some count slackness, but is longsuffering toward us, not willing that any should perish but that all should come to repentance"
(2 Peter 3:9, NKJV).

"No temptation has overtaken you except such as is common to man; but God is faithful, who will not allow you to be tempted beyond what you are able, but with the temptation will also make the way of escape, that you may be able to bear it"
(1 Corinthians 10:13, NKJV).

"For You have delivered my soul from death. Have You not delivered my feet from falling, That I may walk before God In the light of the living?" (Psalm 56:13, NKJV).

Additional Scripture and Promises

Exod. 20:14, 17	*John 8:3–11*	*Eph. 5:3–12*
Gen. 2:24	*Rom. 1:24–32*	*Col. 3:5, 6*
Job 31:1	*Rom. 7:3*	*1 Thess. 4:3–7*
Prov. 5:3–8, 20, 21	*1 Cor. 6:9, 10, 13–20*	*1 Thess. 5:22*
Prov. 6:23–33	*1 Cor. 7:1–16, 37*	*2 Tim. 3:5–7*
Eccles. 7:26	*1 Cor. 10:13*	*Titus 1:15*
Matt. 5:8, 28, 32	*Gal. 5:16–24*	*Heb. 4:15, 16*
Mark 10:11, 12	*Gal. 6:7, 8*	*Heb. 13:4*

STEWARDSHIP

Precious Lord,

You know that I have not always been a good steward of the money, talents, and time You have blessed me with. I have wasted so much. Please forgive me, for my heart is filled with remorse. I truly want to lay up my treasures in the bank of heaven, as You have counseled me to do in Matthew 6:20 and 21.

You declare in Malachi 3:8–10 that I have robbed You when I don't return my tithe, but that if I am a good steward, You will open the windows of heaven and pour out a blessing so huge that I won't have room to receive it! Wow! What a fair and generous God You are! In addition, I know that if I am faithful in using my talents and time to serve You, You have promised in John 12:26 that God will honor me! That's awesome!

Oh, heavenly Father, I seek Your blessings and acknowledge You as my Lord and Savior. You have promised in Philippians 4:19 to meet all of my needs, so help me to trust You more. My heart longs to hear Your words in Matthew 25:23: " ' "Well done, good and faithful servant; you have been faithful over a few things, I will make you ruler over many things. Enter into the joy of your lord" ' " (NKJV).

I claim Your promise in Revelation 17:14 that You will always keep me with You and that I may be among the called, chosen, and faithful. I pray all these things in Jesus' name. Amen.

Promises About Stewardship

" 'But lay up for yourselves treasures in heaven, where neither moth nor rust destroys and where thieves do not break in and steal. For where your treasure is, there your heart will be also' " (Matthew 6:20, 21, NKJV).

" 'Will a man rob God? Yet you have robbed Me! But you say, "In what way have we robbed You?" In tithes and offerings. You are cursed with a curse, for you have robbed Me, even this whole nation. Bring all the tithes into the storehouse, that there may be food in My house, and try Me now in this,' says the LORD of hosts, 'If I will not open for you the windows of heaven and pour out for you such blessing that there will not be room enough to receive it.' " (Malachi 3:8–10, NKJV).

" 'If anyone serves Me, him My Father will honor' " (John 12:26, NKJV).

"My God will meet all your needs according to his glorious riches in Christ Jesus" (Philippians 4:19, NIV).

" 'His lord said to him, "Well done, good and faithful servant; you have been faithful over a few things, I will make you ruler over many things. Enter into the joy of your lord" ' " (Matthew 25:23, NKJV).

" 'These will make war with the Lamb, and the Lamb will overcome them, for He is Lord of lords and King of kings; and those who are with Him are called, chosen, and faithful' " (Revelation 17:14, NKJV).

Additional Scripture and Promises

Deut. 8:18	Prov. 15:16	Matt. 25:21
Deut. 28:2–8, 11, 12	Prov. 22:1, 2,	Luke 6:38
Deut. 29:9	Prov. 22:16, 22	Rom. 13:8
Josh. 1:8	Prov. 28:6, 20, 22	2 Cor. 9:6–8
Ps. 9:18	Eccles. 4:6	Phil. 4:19
Ps. 37:16	Eccles. 5:10–14	1 Tim. 6:7, 17–19
Ps. 41:1	Matt. 6:19–21, 33	Heb. 13:5, 7, 17
Prov. 3:9, 10	Matt. 19:29	

STRENGTH

LOVING FATHER,

Please draw close to me right now because I need strength that only You can give. It seems like everywhere I turn there is nothing but sin, suffering, and death. It is all so discouraging that I feel weary in my soul. I struggle even now for the right words to express accurately how I feel. But then I remember You showed me I didn't need words. You have spoken Your words in Isaiah 41:10 softly into my heart: " ' "Fear not, for I am with you; be not dismayed, for I am your God. I will strengthen you, yes, I will help you, I will uphold you with My righteous right hand" ' " (NKJV).

Oh Father, uphold me with Your righteous right hand! Help me to be patient and wait upon You that I might receive Your strength that is promised in Isaiah 40:31. I'm claiming Your promise in Isaiah 40:29 that You will give strength to the weary and increase the power of the weak. That is definitely what I need in my life right now!

Take away my negative thoughts, and as I hold on to Your promises, let me be flooded with positive feelings. Especially, I ask for Your joy, for in Nehemiah 8:10 You tell me that the joy of the Lord is my strength.

Thank You for Your comfort and encouragement and for once again reminding me in Philippians 4:13 that "I can do all things through Christ who strengthens me" (NKJV). I love You. AMEN.

Promises About Strength

" ' "Fear not, for I am with you; be not dismayed, for I am your God. I will strengthen you, yes, I will help you, I will uphold you with My righteous right hand" ' " (Isaiah 41:10, NKJV).

"But they that wait upon the LORD shall renew their strength; they shall mount up with wings as eagles; they shall run, and not be weary; and they shall walk, and not faint" (Isaiah 40:31, KJV).

"He gives strength to the weary and increases the power of the weak" (Isaiah 40:29, NIV).

" 'Do not sorrow, for the joy of the LORD is your strength' " (Nehemiah 8:10, NKJV).

"I can do all things through Christ who strengthens me" (Philippians 4:13, NKJV).

Additional Scripture and Promises

1 Chron. 16:11	Prov. 10:29	Rom. 5:6
Ps. 18:1, 32–36	Isa. 12:2	1 Cor. 16:13
Ps. 27:1, 14	Isa. 25:4	2 Cor. 3:5
Ps. 28:7, 8	Isa. 26:4	2 Cor. 4:16
Ps. 46:1	Isa. 40:30	2 Cor. 10:3–5
Ps. 118:14	Dan. 10:19	2 Cor. 12:9, 10
Ps. 138:3	Joel 3:10	Heb. 11:33, 34
Ps. 147:5	Rom. 4:20, 21	Rev. 12:10

STRESS

DEAR KIND HEAVENLY FATHER,

I have too much to do—and too many thoughts running around in my head. I'm just plain stressed out and tired of all this busyness. That's why I have come to You, Lord. You have promised in Psalm 55:22 that if I cast all my cares on You, You will sustain me and will not let me fall apart! I want to banish all the anxiety from my heart and let You deal with it because You say in 2 Thessalonians 1:6 and 7 that You'll pay back trouble to those who trouble me—and give me relief. That's good news!

I claim Your promise in Isaiah 26:3 that You will keep me in perfect peace, if I will keep my mind on You and trust in You. Jeremiah 31:25 says You will refresh the weary and satisfy the faint. That's me, Lord. I'm claiming Proverbs 16:3 that if I commit everything to You, my plans will succeed. And finally, there is Your promise in Psalm 37:4 that if my greatest delight is in You, Lord, You will give me the desires of my heart. Thank You! Thank You!

I have so much to look forward to as You work out these things in my life. What an awesome, stress-reducing God You are! In Your name I pray. AMEN.

Promises About Stress

*"Cast your cares on the Lord and he will sustain you;
he will never let the righteous fall" (Psalm 55:22, NIV).*

*"God is just: He will pay back trouble to those who
trouble you and give relief to you who are troubled"
(2 Thessalonians 1:6, 7, NIV).*

*"You will keep in perfect peace him whose mind is steadfast,
because he trusts in you" (Isaiah 26:3, NIV).*

*" 'I will refresh the weary and satisfy the faint' "
(Jeremiah 31:25, NIV).*

*"Commit to the Lord whatever you do,
and your plans will succeed" (Proverbs 16:3, NIV).*

*"Delight yourself in the Lord and he will give you
the desires of your heart" (Psalm 37:4, NIV).*

Additional Scripture and Promises

Exod. 33:14	Prov. 21:5	John 14:1, 27
Ps. 23	Isa. 26:4, 12	1 Cor. 9:24, 25
Ps. 37:8, 9	Isa. 30:15	Eph. 4:26, 27
Ps. 39:6, 7	Nahum 1:7	Phil. 1:6
Ps. 46:1–3, 10	Matt. 6:25, 31–34	Phil. 4:6, 7
Ps. 91:3–7	Matt. 11:28–30	Heb. 4:9–11
Ps. 107:5–7	Mark 4:38–40	1 Pet. 5:7
Prov. 3:26	Luke 12:29–31	

SUCCESS

DEAR FATHER IN HEAVEN,

I come before You asking that You place Your hand of blessing upon my head that my efforts in all I strive for will succeed beyond my wildest expectations! Bless me, Father, and make me prosperous as You have promised in Joshua 1:8 and 9. Lord, I want to be successful in all aspects of my life, whether it is my job, my finances, my relationships, my family, or whatever I am striving to achieve. Please reward me greatly!

Give me the faith that I need to be successful, as You have described in 2 Chronicles 20:20. Thank You for Your promise in Jeremiah 33:3 that if I call to You, You will answer me and show me great and mighty things which I do not know. Oh, my precious Father, I am calling upon You now! I'm excited about Your plans for me because 1 Corinthians 2:9 tells me, " 'Eye has not seen, nor ear heard, nor have entered into the heart of man the things which God has prepared for those who love Him' " (NKJV).

Oh Lord, I love You so very much, and my mind cannot comprehend all the blessings You are waiting to bestow upon me. More importantly, I commit to You all that I do, and I claim Your promise in Proverbs 16:3, believing my plans will succeed. Help me to use every talent and gift You have given me to Your honor and glory! AMEN.

Promises About Success

" 'Do not let this Book of the Law depart from your mouth;
meditate on it day and night, so that you may be careful to do
everything written in it. Then you will be prosperous and
successful. Have I not commanded you? Be strong and courageous.
Do not be terrified; do not be discouraged, for the LORD your God
will be with you wherever you go' " (Joshua 1:8, 9, NIV).

"Early in the morning they left for the Desert of Tekoa.
As they set out, Jehoshaphat stood and said, 'Listen to me,
Judah and people of Jerusalem! Have faith in the LORD your
God and you will be upheld; have faith in his prophets and
you will be successful' " (2 Chronicles 20:20, NIV).

" ' "Call to Me, and I will answer you, and show you great and
mighty things, which you do not know" ' " (Jeremiah 33:3, NKJV).

" 'Eye has not seen, nor ear heard, nor have entered into
the heart of man the things which God has prepared
for those who love Him' " (1 Corinthians 2:9, NKJV).

"Commit to the LORD whatever you do,
and your plans will succeed" (Proverbs 16:3, NIV).

Additional Scripture and Promises

THANKFULNESS

DEAR HOLY GOD AND CREATOR OF THE UNIVERSE,

Thank You, loving Father, for all the wonderful things You have done for me. You are such a kind and generous God, so full of grace and mercy! May I always remember that every good thing is from You. You have blessed me so much and there are not enough words to express my love and gratitude for the awesome God that You are. Philippians 4:6 tells me that every request I make to You should be made with thanksgiving. Help me not to just come to You asking for things. Lord, let me always remember to thank You and give You praise.

I claim Your promise in Philippians 4:7 that if I do this, "the peace of God, which transcends all understanding, will guard [my heart] and [my mind] in Christ Jesus" (NIV), even though I'm experiencing trials and suffering. Regardless what happens, Lord, I know I can always choose to thank You for trusting me with these experiences. I am assured that I will not be overcome, discouraged, or negative. I want Psalm 100 to be my guide: "He . . . has made us, . . . We are His people . . . Enter into His gates with thanksgiving, . . . For the LORD is good; His mercy is everlasting, And His truth endures to all generations" (NKJV).

And may Ephesians 5:20 be my motto, "Giving thanks always for all things" (NKJV). Precious Father, whatever is happening in my life, even in the bad times, please make me thankful! AMEN.

Promises About Thankfulness

"Do not be anxious about anything, but in everything, by prayer and petition, with thanksgiving, present your requests to God. And the peace of God, which transcends all understanding, will guard your hearts and your minds in Christ Jesus"
(Philippians 4:6, 7, NIV).

"Make a joyful shout to the LORD, all you lands! Serve the LORD with gladness; come before His presence with singing. Know that the LORD, He is God; it is He who has made us, and not we ourselves; we are His people and the sheep of His pasture. Enter into His gates with thanksgiving, and into His courts with praise. Be thankful to Him, and bless His name. For the LORD is good; His mercy is everlasting, and His truth endures to all generations"
(Psalm 100, NKJV).

"Giving thanks always for all things to God the Father in the name of our Lord Jesus Christ"
(Ephesians 5:20, NKJV).

Additional Scripture and Promises

1 Sam. 12:24	*Ps. 86:15*	*1 Cor. 15:57, 58*
Ps. 13:6	*Ps. 107:1, 2 , 8, 9*	*2 Cor. 2:14*
Ps. 26:7	*Ps. 107:21, 22*	*2 Cor. 4:15*
Ps. 28:7	*Ps. 111:4*	*2 Cor. 9:11–15*
Ps. 29:2	*Ps. 116:2, 17*	*Eph. 5:19*
Ps. 50:14	*Ps. 147:7*	*Phil. 4:4*
Ps. 65:9–11	*Dan. 2:23*	*Col. 4:2*
Ps. 68:19	*Jonah 2:9*	*1 Thess. 5:18*
Ps. 69:30	*Matt. 11:25*	

THOUGHTS

DEAR FATHER IN HEAVEN,

I praise You for who You are! Your greatness and goodness are above understanding. I want to sing with David in Psalm 139:17, "How precious also are Your thoughts to me, O God! How great is the sum of them!" (NKJV). Lord, You know me so intimately. You knew me before I was born. You know the number of hairs on my head. And as Psalm 94:11 says, You even know the thoughts I'm thinking. I realize there is nothing I can hide from You!

Oh precious Savior, send Your Holy Spirit to keep my mind on the uplifting things mentioned in Philippians 4:8—those things that are true, noble, just, pure, lovely, and of a good report. Oh Lord, forgive me for dwelling on sinful things and please remove any negativity from my mind. Instead of thinking the worst about myself and others, let me think only positive thoughts. I want the Spirit-controlled mind that Paul speaks of in Romans 8:6 because it results in life and peace, while the sinful mind ends in death.

Lord, help me to have the willpower necessary to follow Your counsel in Romans 12:2 to be transformed by the renewing of my mind. Thank You for answering my prayer. In Jesus' name. AMEN.

Promises About Thoughts

"How precious also are Your thoughts to me, O God! How great is the sum of them!" (Psalm 139:17, NKJV).

"The LORD knows the thoughts of man; he knows that they are futile" (Psalm 94:11, NIV).

"Finally, brethren, whatever things are true, whatever things are noble, whatever things are just, whatever things are pure, whatever things are lovely, whatever things are of good report, if there is any virtue and if there is anything praiseworthy— meditate on these things" (Philippians 4:8, NKJV).

"The mind of sinful man is death, but the mind controlled by the Spirit is life and peace" (Romans 8:6, NIV).

"Be transformed by the renewing of your mind. Then you will be able to test and approve what God's will is—his good, pleasing and perfect will" (Romans 12:2, NIV).

Additional Scripture and Promises

1 Chron. 28:9	Isa. 26:3	Matt. 15:19
Ps. 10:4	Isa. 55:7, 8	Rom. 8:5
Ps. 51:10	Jer. 17:10	Rom. 12:3
Ps. 139:2, 17–24	Jer. 29:11	2 Cor. 10:4, 5
Prov. 12:5	Micah 4:12	Gal. 6:3
Prov. 15:26	Matt. 5:8, 28	Eph. 3:20
Prov. 16:3	Matt. 9:4	Heb. 4:12
Prov. 23:7	Matt. 12:34	

TIME

DEAR LOVING FATHER,

I'm constantly trying to do more things than I can possibly pack into one day—and I never have enough time. Like Job, in Job 7:6, I lament, " 'My days are swifter than a weaver's shuttle' " (NKJV)!

Thank You for the reminder in Ecclesiastes 3:1, "To everything there is a season, and a time to every purpose under the heaven" (NKJV). Now I realize that *time* is not the problem. You've given me enough time to do the things You want me to do. The problem is me and how I'm using that time.

Lord, thank You for loving me just because I exist! I know, as Psalm 89:47 says, that my days are short here on this earth, but it's not what I accomplish that counts, it's my relationship with You. You have said in 2 Peter 3:8 that a thousand years in Your sight are like a day that has just gone by or like a watch in the night.

I believe time is a talent You've given me. Help me to use it to honor and glorify You—to praise Your holy name. I love the thought in Ecclesiastes 3:11 that You have made "everything beautiful in its time" (NIV). Help me to use my time to draw so close to You that Your character shines out beautifully in my life. I love You so much. In Jesus' name. AMEN.

PROMISES ABOUT TIME

" 'My days are swifter than a weaver's shuttle' "
(Job 7:6, NKJV).

"To everything there is a season,
a time for every purpose under heaven"
(Ecclesiastes 3:1, NKJV).

"Remember how short my time is"
(Psalm 89:47, NKJV).

"Do not forget this one thing, dear friends:
With the Lord a day is like a thousand years,
and a thousand years are like a day"
(2 Peter 3:8, NIV).

"[God] has made everything beautiful in its time.
He has also set eternity in the hearts of men; yet they
cannot fathom what God has done from beginning to end"
(Ecclesiastes 3:11, NIV).

ADDITIONAL SCRIPTURE AND PROMISES

Job 7:1	Eccles. 3:1–7, 17	Rom. 13:11, 12
Job 24:1	Hosea 10:12	2 Cor. 6:1, 2
Ps. 69:13	Matt. 6:33	James 4:14
Ps. 90:4, 9–12	Mark 13:33	
Ps. 119:126	John 7:6	
Prov. 27:1	Acts 1:7	

TITHE

Dear Precious Savior and Creator God,

I know that everything belongs to You. Without You there wouldn't be galaxies of stars, oceans full of sea creatures, soaring birds, endless forests, wild animals, jungles, or towering mountain peaks. Father God, You own everything, even the property that I have title to and the paycheck that I cash. Then, why is it, Lord, that sometimes I'm reluctant to give You back a small portion of what You have given me?

I realize that 10 percent of my income does not belong to me. Lord, I don't want to steal from You! Leviticus 27:30 says that tithe is holy to You. But as important as tithing is, don't let me be like the hypocrites in Matthew 23:23 who were guilty of legalistically paying tithe while neglecting the "weightier matters of the law" such as justice, mercy, and faith!

Before I spend anything on myself, I want to be a cheerful giver of the tenth that is Yours. Malachi 3:8–11 makes it clear that if I honor my obligation to You, You will throw open the floodgates of heaven and pour out so much blessing that I will not have room enough for it—and You'll even protect my possessions. Wow! What an incredible promise! I claim that! Thank You for being such a generous, awesome God. Amen.

Promises About Tithe

" ' "And all the tithe of the land, whether of the seed of the land or of the fruit of the tree, is the Lord's. It is holy to the Lord" ' "
(Leviticus 27:30, NKJV).

" 'Woe to you, scribes and Pharisees, hypocrites! For you pay tithe of mint and anise and cummin, and have neglected the weightier matters of the law: justice and mercy and faith. These you ought to have done, without leaving the others undone' "
(Matthew 23:23, NKJV).

"So let each one give as he purposes in his heart, not grudgingly or of necessity; for God loves a cheerful giver"
(2 Corinthians 9:7, NKJV).

" 'Will a man rob God? Yet you rob me. But you ask, "How do we rob you?" In tithes and offerings. You are under a curse—the whole nation of you—because you are robbing me. Bring the whole tithe into the storehouse, that there may be food in my house. Test me in this,' says the Lord Almighty, 'and see if I will not throw open the floodgates of heaven and pour out so much blessing that you will not have room enough for it. I will prevent pests from devouring your crops, and the vines in your fields will not cast their fruit,' says the Lord Almighty"
(Malachi 3:8–11, NIV).

Additional Scripture and Promises

Gen. 14:18–20	Ps. 116:12	Luke 18:12
Gen. 28:20–22	Prov. 3:9	Acts 20:35
Num. 18:21, 24	Matt. 6:20	1 Cor. 9:13
Deut. 14:22	Matt. 10:8	2 Cor. 9:6
2 Chron. 31:5, 12	Mark 12:17	Heb. 7:1, 2
Neh. 13:12	Luke 6:38	James 1:17
Ps. 96:8	Luke 12:48	

TRIALS

Trial

MY DEAR HEAVENLY FATHER,

I feel overwhelmed with all the problems I'm facing. I don't mean to complain, Lord, because I know You went through terrible trials, and that as Romans 8:18 says, my present sufferings aren't worth anything compared with the future glory I'll have with You. So, Lord, I turn to Your Word for direction.

In Romans 12:12, You tell me to be joyful in hope, patient in affliction, and faithful in prayer. I want that so much, Lord. But I realize that I can't have that kind of positive attitude when I'm down, unless You give it to me. So please Father, help me to be joyful in hope, patient in affliction, and faithful in prayer.

Thank You for promising in 1 Corinthians 10:13 that You won't let anything come to me that I can't bear—that You will help me cope or provide a way of escape. In James 1:1–4 You say that I should consider trials an opportunity for joy, for when my faith is tested, my endurance will grow and I'll be strong in character and ready for anything.

So, Lord, I praise You for my trials that will strengthen my character! I claim the promise in 1 Peter 5:10 that after I suffer a little while, You will restore me and make me strong, firm, and steadfast. Thank You, Jesus. AMEN.

PROMISES ABOUT TRIALS

"I consider that our present sufferings are not worth comparing with the glory that will be revealed in us" (Romans 8:18, NIV).

"Be joyful in hope, patient in affliction, faithful in prayer" (Romans 12:12, NIV).

"No temptation has seized you except what is common to man. And God is faithful; he will not let you be tempted beyond what you can bear. But when you are tempted, he will also provide a way out so that you can stand up under it" (1 Corinthians 10:13, NIV).

"Dear brothers and sisters, when troubles come your way, consider it an opportunity for great joy. For you know that when your faith is tested, your endurance has a chance to grow. So let it grow, for when your endurance is fully developed, you will be perfect and complete, needing nothing" (James 1:1–4, NLT).

"The God of all grace, who called you to his eternal glory in Christ, after you have suffered a little while, will himself restore you and make you strong, firm and steadfast" (1 Peter 5:10, NIV).

ADDITIONAL SCRIPTURE AND PROMISES

1 Sam. 26:24	Ps. 34:17–19	Lam. 3:32, 33
Job 1:21, 22	Ps. 55:22	Dan. 12:10
Job 2:10	Ps. 66:10–12	Zech. 13:9
Job 42:10–12	Ps. 91:14, 15	John 14:1
Job 5:17	Ps. 138:7	John 16:33
Job 23:10	Prov. 3:11, 12	Rom. 5:3
Ps. 9:9	Prov. 17:3	1 Pet. 4:12–14
Ps. 23:4	Isa. 43:1–3	
Ps. 32:7	Isa. 48:10	

TROUBLE

Dear Lord,

I'm going through a really tough time right now. And I have no idea how I'm going to get out of this mess. So I really, really need You to rescue me as You assure me You know how to do in 2 Peter 2:9 and that You *will* do in Psalm 34:19. I claim Your promise in Psalm 91:14 and 15 that if I love You and call upon Your name, You'll be with me in trouble and will deliver me.

Lord, I love You, and in Your holy name, I ask You to help me. In fact, I'm pleading with You to fulfill Psalm 40:1–3 in my life. Hear my cry; get me out of this horrible pit and the miry clay that's dragging me down, and set my feet on a solid rock.

I claim Psalm 18:2 that You, oh Lord, are my Rock, my Fortress, my Deliverer, my God, my Strength, my Shield, the Horn of my Salvation, and my Stronghold.

I praise You in advance, Lord, for completing Your rescue operation that You have promised in Psalm 40 by establishing my steps—telling me what I should do—and putting a song in my heart, a song of praise and joy that others can look at my life and glorify You because of what You've done for me. I love You so much! Thank You for being my Savior. Amen.

Promises About Trouble

"The Lord knows how to rescue godly men from trials"
(2 Peter 2:9, NIV).

"A righteous man may have many troubles, but the LORD
delivers him from them all" (Psalm 34:19, NIV).

" 'Because he loves me,' says the LORD, 'I will rescue him; I will
protect him, for he acknowledges my name. He will call upon
me, and I will answer him; I will be with him in trouble, I will
deliver him and honor him' " (Psalm 91:14, 15, NIV).

"I waited patiently for the LORD; And He inclined to me,
And heard my cry. He also brought me up out of a horrible pit,
Out of the miry clay, And set my feet upon a rock,
And established my steps. He has put a new song in my mouth—
Praise to our God; Many will see it and fear,
And will trust in the LORD"
(Psalm 40:1–3, NKJV).

"The LORD is my rock and my fortress and my deliverer;
My God, my strength, in whom I will trust;
My shield and the horn of my salvation, my stronghold"
(Psalm 18:2, NKJV).

Additional Scripture and Promises

Deut. 4:30, 31	*Ps. 77:2*	*John 16:33*
Neh. 9:27	*Ps. 86:7*	*1 Cor. 10:13*
Job 5:19	*Ps. 91*	*2 Cor. 1:3, 4*
Job 13:15	*Ps. 121:2*	*2 Cor. 4:17*
Ps. 9:9	*Ps. 138:7*	*2 Tim. 3:12*
Ps. 22:11	*Isa. 33:2*	*James 1:1–3, 12*
Ps. 27:5	*Jer. 39:17*	*1 Pet. 4:12–14*
Ps. 37:39, 40	*Nahum 1:7*	
Ps. 50:15	*John 14:1*	

TRUTH

My Father in Heaven,

When I spend time with You in Your Word, it's easy to see truth. It's when I don't want to give up my own opinions, desires, or the traditions I've grown up with that I struggle with what's right and wrong. I feel as if I'm in a daily battle with self. I'm tired of hanging on to my sins, and I ache to be free. You have promised in John 8:32, " 'You shall know the truth and the truth shall set you free' " (NKJV).

Jesus, in John 14:6, You have said that You are the Way, the Truth, and the Life. I hold fast to this assurance, and I ask You to come into my heart right now and reveal Yourself to me. I lay my sins at Your feet and claim Psalm 145:18, that You are near to all who call upon You in truth. You say in Matthew 7:7 that if I seek, I'll find. That's why I believe You'll continue to reveal truth to me if I keep studying Your Word. For 2 Timothy 3:16 says that all Scripture is profitable for doctrine, reproof, correction, and instruction in righteousness.

Oh God, there is so much error in this world. Satan is so subtle in his deceptions. I need You to help me discern truth from error. Convict me when I'm wrong. And then, Lord, give me the willpower to take a stand for truth. Thank You for all Your precious promises and for hearing and answering my prayer. Amen.

PROMISES ABOUT TRUTH

"Then Jesus said to those Jews who believed Him, 'If you abide in My word, you are My disciples indeed. And you shall know the truth, and the truth shall make you free' "
(John 8:31, 32, NKJV).

"Jesus answered, 'I am the way and the truth and the life. No one comes to the Father except through me' "
(John 14:6, NIV).

"The LORD is near to all who call upon Him, to all who call upon Him in truth" (Psalm 145:18, NKJV).

" 'Ask, and it will be given to you; seek, and you will find; knock, and it will be opened to you' " (Matthew 7:7, NKJV).

"All Scripture is given by inspiration of God, and is profitable for doctrine, for reproof, for correction, for instruction in righteousness" (2 Timothy 3:16, NKJV).

ADDITIONAL SCRIPTURE AND PROMISES

VALUES & PRIORITIES

My Father in Heaven,

It's so easy to get caught up in worldly things and begin thinking that being popular, rich, successful, and powerful is important. But Lord, I know better. Your Word tells me in Colossians 3:2 to think on things above, not on earthly things. Jesus says in Matthew 6:33 that if I seek first the kingdom of God and His righteousness, *everything else will be added*. What a wonderful promise! Your Word clearly tells me what my values should be.

Proverbs 22:1 tells me a good name is more important than riches, and loving favor is better than silver and gold. You have counseled me in 1 Corinthians 12:31 and 13:13 to earnestly desire the best gifts, the greatest gift being love. May Your promises in Romans 12:2 and Proverbs 21:21 shape my value system. You say that if I don't conform to the lifestyle of this world, but instead pursue righteousness and love, then I will be able to discern Your good, pleasing, and perfect will and find life, prosperity, and honor.

Oh Lord, help me to get my priorities straight! Help my values to reflect Yours. Help me to keep my eyes so focused on You that I won't be tempted to spend my time, talents, and money on things that have no eternal value. Once again, I commit my life, my thoughts, my words, and my actions to You. I want to make You my highest priority. I love You, Lord. Amen.

Promises About Values & Priorities

"Set your mind on things above, not on things on the earth"
(Colossians 3:2, NKJV).

" 'But seek first the kingdom of God and His righteousness, and all
these things shall be added to you' " (Matthew 6:33, NKJV).

"A good name is to be chosen rather than great riches, loving
favor rather than silver and gold" (Proverbs 22:1, NKJV).

"But earnestly desire the best gifts. And yet I show you
a more excellent way. . . . And now abide faith, hope, love,
these three; but the greatest of these is love"
(1 Corinthians 12:31; 13:13, NKJV).

"Do not conform any longer to the pattern of this world, but be
transformed by the renewing of your mind. Then you will be
able to test and approve what God's will is—his good, pleasing
and perfect will" (Romans 12:2, NIV).

"He who pursues righteousness and love finds life, prosperity and
honor" (Proverbs 21:21, NIV).

Additional Scripture and Promises

Deut. 8:11–14
Josh. 24:15
1 Chron. 16:11, 12
Ps. 84:10, 11
Prov. 22:4
Prov. 23:4, 5
Eccles. 3:1–8, 11
Eccles. 12:13

Jer. 9:23, 24
Micah 6:8
Matt. 6:20–24, 31–33
Matt. 16:24, 25
Matt. 20:26–28
Luke 9:23–25
Luke 12:15
Luke 14:1, 7–14

Acts 20:24
2 Cor. 5:9
Phil. 4:8
Col. 1:10
2 Tim. 2:22
James 4:10

VICTORY
OVER TEMPTATION

DEAR ALMIGHTY GOD,

You know what's happening in my life—the struggles and temptations. Just when I think I'm winning, down I go again. I'm on a losing streak with the devil! But Lord, You also know my heart and how very much I want to be victorious. So Jesus, my Savior and victorious King, I'm giving my battle to You. I believe the words of 1 Corinthians 15:57 will be fulfilled in my life: "Thanks be to God! He gives us the victory through our Lord Jesus Christ" (NIV).

John 16:33 tells me that although I can't escape trouble, I can take heart and have peace because You have already overcome the world. That's good news—and it gives me hope! I claim the promise in Proverbs 21:30 and 31 that no wisdom, no insight, no plan can succeed against You. Satan may be ready to do battle against me, but I am assured that victory rests with You. I believe You're saying to me what You told King Jehoshaphat in 2 Chronicles 20:15, " ' "the battle is not yours, but God's" ' " (NKJV). Hallelujah!

Lord, do what You say You'll do in Psalm 60:12— "trample down [my] enemies" (NIV)! I claim the promise of Romans 16:20 that You will bruise Satan under my feet. Wow! I'm so thankful that You are my Lord and Savior, and Almighty God! Thank You, Jesus, for giving me the assurance that with You I can have victory over the devil! Praise Your holy name! AMEN.

PROMISES ABOUT VICTORY OVER TEMPTATION

"Thanks be to God! He gives us the victory through our Lord Jesus Christ" (1 Corinthians 15:57, NIV).

" 'I have told you these things, so that in me you may have peace. In this world you will have trouble. But take heart! I have overcome the world' " (John 16:33, NIV).

"There is no wisdom, no insight, no plan that can succeed against the LORD. The horse is made ready for the day of battle, but victory rests with the LORD" (Proverbs 21:30, 31, NIV).

" ' "Do not be afraid nor dismayed because of this great multitude, for the battle is not yours, but God's" ' " (2 Chronicles 20:15, NKJV).

"With God we will gain the victory, and he will trample down our enemies" (Psalm 60:12, NIV).

"And the God of peace shall bruise Satan under your feet shortly. The grace of our Lord Jesus Christ be with you. Amen" (Romans 16:20, KJV).

ADDITIONAL SCRIPTURE AND PROMISES

2 Chron. 20:17	*Rom. 6:17, 18*	*Phil. 4:13*
Ps. 119:101–104	*Rom. 8:37*	*Heb. 2:17, 18*
Ps. 121:2, 7	*Rom. 12:21*	*Heb. 7:25*
Ps. 141:3, 4	*1 Cor. 10:12, 13*	*James 1:2, 12–15*
Prov. 4:14, 15	*2 Cor. 2:14*	*1 John 2:15–17*
Matt. 6:13	*2 Cor. 12:9*	*1 John 5:3–5*
Matt. 26:41	*Eph. 4:26*	*Jude 24*
Mark 14:38	*Eph. 6:10–13*	*Rev. 3:10*

WISDOM

Dear Heavenly Father,

You are the Source of all true wisdom, and I need that wisdom right now. You know what I'm facing and how easy it would be for me to make a mistake. Proverbs 3:7 warns me against thinking I'm smart enough to know what to say or do by myself or that I have a good enough memory to recall the essential facts that are so important to understanding. That's why I'm claiming the promise in James 1:5 that if anyone lacks wisdom and will ask You, You will give it liberally.

Lord, I'm pleading with You to give me Your wisdom—to impress me with insight from the Holy Spirit. In Proverbs 4:11 and 12, You promise to guide me in the way of wisdom and lead me along straight paths so I won't stumble. Thank You, Lord, for this insight.

My desire is to follow Your counsel in Proverbs 2:1–5 to continually look for wisdom as I would for silver or hidden treasure, for when I do, You have promised that I will find "the knowledge of God." I know You will answer my prayer as You did for King Solomon so long ago. Thank You for always being there for me. I love You, Lord. Amen.

Promises About Wisdom

"Do not be wise in your own eyes" (Proverbs 3:7, NKJV).

"If any of you lacks wisdom, he should ask God,
who gives generously to all without finding fault,
and it will be given to him" (James 1:5, NIV).

"I will guide you in the way of wisdom and lead you along
straight paths. When you walk, your steps will not be hampered;
when you run, you will not stumble"
(Proverbs 4:11, 12, NIV).

"If you accept my words and store up my commands within you,
turning your ear to wisdom and applying your heart to under-
standing, and if you call out for insight and cry aloud for
understanding, and if you look for it as for silver and search for
it as for hidden treasure, then you will understand the fear of the
LORD and find the knowledge of God" (Proverbs 2:1–5, NIV).

"And God gave Solomon wisdom and exceedingly great
understanding, and largeness of heart like the sand on the
seashore. Thus Solomon's wisdom excelled the wisdom of
all the men of the East and all the wisdom of Egypt.
For he was wiser than all men" (1 Kings 4:29–31, NKJV).

Additional Scripture and Promises

Job 32:8, 9	Prov. 19:8, 20	1 Cor. 3:18–20
Ps. 16:7	Prov. 26:12	2 Cor. 4:6
Ps. 19:7, 8	Eccles. 2:26	Phil. 1:9–11
Ps. 119:73, 98–100, 130	Jer. 33:2, 3	Col. 1:9
Prov. 1:7	Dan. 12:3	Col. 2:2, 3
Prov. 4:6–9	Matt. 10:16	James 3:13
Prov. 15:24	1 Cor. 1:5, 20, 25, 30	2 Pet. 1:2
Prov. 16:16, 20	1 Cor. 2:10–12	2 Pet. 3:18

WITNESSING

Precious Lord,

When I think of Your incredible sacrifice for my salvation, how can I keep this lifesaving news to myself? You are such an awesome God! Please fill my heart full to overflowing with Your passionate love for souls. I want to be a mighty soul-winning tool and not miss even one opportunity to witness for You—even though I feel inadequate.

Lord, I need insight and boldness from the Holy Spirit! I'm scared I won't know what to say. That's why I'm claiming the promise in Acts 1:8 that You will fill me with Your Holy Spirit, just as You did the apostles at Pentecost.

Peter says in 1 Peter 3:15 that we should always be prepared to give an answer to those who ask about our faith. But no matter how much I study, I don't think I'll ever know enough! So give me courage to speak out anyway, claiming the promise in Jeremiah 33:3 that if I call upon You, You will answer and give me words that are above and beyond my own understanding.

Now with joy and a sense of adventure, I will follow Your commission in Mark 16:15 to " 'Go into all the world' " (NIV)—or at least go into my own little world—and tell others about You.

So, please, Lord, bring me someone today who needs to know how much You love them. Give me a divine appointment today! Thank You for giving me this awesome privilege. I love You, my Lord and my God. Amen.

Promises About Witnessing

" 'But you shall receive power when the Holy Spirit
has come upon you; and you shall be witnesses to Me
in Jerusalem, and in all Judea and Samaria,
and to the end of the earth' " (Acts 1:8, NJKV).

"In your hearts set apart Christ as Lord.
Always be prepared to give an answer to everyone
who asks you to give the reason for the hope that you
have. But do this with gentleness and respect"
(1 Peter 3:15, NIV).

" ' "Call to Me, and I will answer you,
and show you great and mighty things,
which you do not know" ' "
(Jeremiah 33:3, NKJV).

"He said to them, 'Go into all the world and
preach the good news to all creation' "
(Mark 16:15, NIV).

Additional Scripture and Promises

Ps. 40:16	Matt. 7:20	Acts 18:26
Ps. 66:16	Matt. 10:19, 32	2 Cor. 5:20
Ps. 105:1, 2	Matt. 28:18–20	Eph. 6:10, 13–15
Isa. 50:4	Mark 8:38	Eph. 6:18–20
Isa. 52:7	Mark 16:15–20	2 Tim. 2:15, 16, 23–25
Jer. 1:7–9	Luke 12:8, 9, 12	Philem. 6
Zech. 8:16	Luke 21:14, 15	James 5:19, 20
Matt. 5:14–16	John 20:21	1 Pet. 3:8–11, 16

WORDS

DEAR HEAVENLY FATHER,

My prayer is that You will "Set a watch . . . before my mouth; [and] keep the door of my lips" as Psalm 141:3 (KJV) says, so I won't say things that I'll be sorry for later. Words are so powerful. They can either lift spirits and inspire excellence, or they can tear down and destroy. As Proverbs 18:21 puts it, they can cause "Death and life" (KJV).

Oh Lord, I want to be an encourager and bring life to people. I want my words to help—not hurt. That's why I want to follow the instruction in Ephesians 4:29: "Do not let any unwholesome talk come out of your mouths, but only what is helpful for building others up according to their needs, that it may benefit those who listen" (NIV). Oh Lord, I have failed so often. Forgive me. I don't mean to say things that hurt others. Luke 6:45 says that our speech comes from what's inside our hearts. I know that means I've got to be careful to not harbor negative emotions.

Dear Lord, help me put off anger, wrath, malice, blasphemy, and filthy language. Instead, I want to make sure my words are seasoned with grace. Only with Your help, Lord Jesus, can I conquer my tongue. Help me, please. AMEN.

Promises About Words

"Set a watch, O Lord, before my mouth; keep the door of my lips" (Psalm 141:3, KJV).

"Death and life are in the power of the tongue: and they that love it shall eat the fruit thereof" (Proverbs 18:21, KJV).

"Do not let any unwholesome talk come out of your mouths, but only what is helpful for building others up according to their needs, that it may benefit those who listen" (Ephesians 4:29, NIV).

"'A good man out of the good treasure of his heart brings forth good; and an evil man out of the evil treasure of his heart brings forth evil. For out of the abundance of the heart his mouth speaks'" (Luke 6:45, NKJV).

"But now you yourselves are to put off all these: anger, wrath, malice, blasphemy, filthy language out of your mouth" (Colossians 3:8, NKJV).

Additional Scripture and Promises

Job 19:2	*Matt. 12:34–37*	*1 Tim. 4:12*
Job 27:3, 4	*1 Cor. 13:1*	*2 Tim. 2:14*
Ps. 19:14	*2 Cor. 13:10*	*Titus 3:9*
Prov. 10:12, 19, 31, 32	*Eph. 4:29–32*	*James 1:19, 26*
Prov. 12:18, 19, 25	*Eph. 5:4*	*James 3:2, 6–11*
Prov. 15:1–4, 23–28	*Phil. 2:14*	*1 Pet. 3:10*
Eccles. 5:2, 3	*Col. 4:6*	
Eccles. 10:12, 14	*1 Thess. 4:18*	

WORK

DEAR FATHER IN HEAVEN,

What career path do You want me to take? What do You want me to do for You? I want to enjoy my work, because it's Your gift to me. Psalm 37:23 says that "The steps of a good man are ordered by the LORD" (NKJV). I just wish You would light up a burning bush or send a flash of light as You did when You wanted Moses and Paul to change directions! Lord, I need to know what decision to make!

I'm praying that Your Word will give me the guidance I'm seeking to be successful in my lifework. You have said in 2 Timothy 3:16 and 17 that Scripture is Your way of preparing us and fully equipping us for every good thing You want us to do. Help me to study and patiently wait for Your plan to be revealed to me.

I realize that commitment is essential, for Proverbs 16:3 says, "Commit to the LORD whatever you do, and your plans will succeed" (NIV). I commit whatever work I do to You, and with Your help, will work hard and cheerfully as You have commissioned me to do in Colossians 3:23.

Thank You, Lord, for promising in 2 Corinthians 9:8 that I will always have everything I need and plenty left over to share with others. May Your favor rest upon me and establish the work of my hands—whatever that may be. Lord, I am trusting You to direct my paths! AMEN.

Promises About Work

"The steps of a good man are ordered by the LORD, and He delights in his way" (Psalm 37:23, NKJV).

"All Scripture is inspired by God and is useful to teach us what is true and to make us realize what is wrong in our lives. It corrects us when we are wrong and teaches us to do what is right. God uses it to prepare and equip his people to do every good work" (2 Timothy 3:16, 17, NLT).

"Commit to the LORD whatever you do, and your plans will succeed" (Proverbs 16:3, NIV).

"Work willingly at whatever you do, as though you were working for the Lord rather than for people" (Colossians 3:23, NLT).

"And God will generously provide all you need. Then you will always have everything you need and plenty left over to share with others" (2 Corinthians 9:8, NLT).

Additional Scripture and Promises

Exod. 20:9
2 Chron. 15:7
Neh. 4:6
Ps. 128:2
Prov. 6:6
Prov. 12:11, 24
Prov. 13:4, 11, 14, 23
Prov. 31:27

Eccles. 12:14
Ezek. 16:49
Matt. 16:27
Luke 10:7
John 6:27
Rom. 12:11
1 Cor. 15:58
Gal. 6:4

Eph. 4:11–16
Col. 3:2, 24
1 Tim. 5:8
2 Tim. 2:6, 20, 21
Heb. 6:10
Rev. 14:13
Rev. 22:12

WORRY

Dear Heavenly Father,

I know You have promised in Philippians 4:19 to supply all my needs. And yet when things get tough, as they are right now, I worry about my problems. Thank You for the instruction in 1 Peter 5:7 that I should give You my worries because You care what's happening to me. Lord, I'm handing them over right now.

I'm also claiming the promise in Luke 12:22–31 that if I seek Your kingdom—instead of worrying about my own little world—that all the things I need, like food and clothing, will be given to me as well. That's an incredible promise! Thank You, Lord!

Not only do I seek Your kingdom, but I invite You to live in my heart and mind, so my negative thoughts will be transformed into Your positive thoughts and I'll experience Your peace, as You have promised me in Philippians 4:5–7. In Proverbs 16:3, You say that if I commit my plans to You, they will succeed! Lord, take my plans and fill me with hope—instead of worry—about the incredible future You've promised me.

And thank You for the promise in Romans 8:28 that everything will work out. I'm really holding on to that! *I love You Lord!* Amen.

PROMISES ABOUT WORRY

"And my God shall supply all our need according to His riches in glory by Christ Jesus" (Philippians 4:19, NKJV).

"Give all your worries and cares to God, for he cares about you" (1 Peter 5:7, NLT).

"Then Jesus said . . . 'do not worry about your life, what you will eat; or about your body, what you will wear. Life is more than food, and the body more than clothes. . . . . But seek his kingdom, and these things will be given to you as well' " (Luke 12:22–31, NIV).

"The Lord is near. Do not be anxious about anything, but in everything, by prayer and petition, with thanksgiving, present your requests to God. And the peace of God, which transcends all understanding, will guard your hearts and your minds in Christ Jesus" (Philippians 4:5–7, NIV).

"Commit to the Lord whatever you do, and your plans will succeed" (Proverbs 16:3, NIV).

"And we know that all things work together for good to those that love God, to those who are the called according to His purpose" (Romans 8:28, NKJV).

ADDITIONAL SCRIPTURE AND PROMISES

Deut. 4:30, 31	*Ps. 40:1–3*	*Prov. 11:8, 17*
Deut. 31:8	*Ps. 43:5*	*Prov. 12:25*
Josh. 1:5	*Ps. 46:1–3*	*Jer. 39:17*
Job 5:19	*Ps. 55:22*	*Nahum 1:7*
Ps. 23	*Ps. 56:3*	*Matt. 6:27–33*
Ps. 32:7	*Ps. 59:16*	*John 14:1, 27*
Ps. 34:4, 17–19	*Ps. 60:11*	*2 Cor. 1:3, 4*
Ps. 37:39, 40	*Ps. 91*	*1 Pet. 5:10*

WORSHIP

ALMIGHTY FATHER GOD,

What an awesome and magnificent God You are! I bow humbly before You with respect, awe, and recognition that You alone are the God of the universe! As Psalm 29:2 says, I worship You in the beauty of Your holiness. You are great, Lord, and Your understanding is infinite. Your way is perfect.

I try to imagine the majesty of Your throne in heaven as Isaiah saw it in Isaiah 6. You are high and lifted up and the train of Your robe fills the temple. And above Your throne are the seraphim—each with six wings—crying out, " 'Holy, holy, holy is the LORD of hosts; the whole earth is full of His glory!' " (NKJV).

Oh Lord, my God, I am not worthy to be in Your presence, and yet You have promised in James 4:8 that as I draw closer to You, You will draw closer to me. So as I'm admonished to do in Hebrews 4:16, I come boldly to Your throne of grace, praising Your holy name forever!

I worship You right now, as I'm encouraged to do in Psalm 100. With a joyful shout and with singing I come before Your presence, with thanksgiving and praise on my lips. For Lord, You are good. Your mercy is everlasting. And Your truth endures to all generations. Praise be to You. AMEN.

Promises About Worship

"Give unto the LORD the glory due to His name; worship the LORD in the beauty of holiness" (Psalm 29:2, NKJV).

"I saw the Lord sitting on a throne, high and lifted up, and the train of His robe filled the temple. Above it stood seraphim; each one had six wings: with two he covered his face, with two he covered his feet, and with two he flew. And one cried to another and said: 'Holy, holy, holy is the LORD of hosts; The whole earth is full of His glory!' " (Isaiah 6:1–3, NKJV).

"Draw near to God and He will draw near to you" (James 4:8, NKJV).

"Let us therefore come boldly to the throne of grace, that we may obtain mercy and find grace to help in time of need" (Hebrews 4:16, NKJV).

"Make a joyful shout to the LORD . . . Come before His presence with singing. . . . Enter into His gates with thanksgiving, And into His courts with praise. . . .For the LORD is good; His mercy is everlasting, And His truth endures to all generations" (Psalm 100, NKJV).

Additional Scripture and Promises

Lev. 19:30	*Ps. 98:4–6*	*Matt. 15:8, 9*
1 Chron. 16:29	*Ps. 99:5, 9*	*Luke 4:16*
Ps. 5:7	*Ps. 112:1*	*Rom. 15:5, 6*
Ps. 63:3–5	*Eccles. 5:1, 2*	*1 Tim. 1:17*
Ps. 66:1, 4	*Isa. 56:7*	*Heb. 10:25*
Ps. 77:12	*Isa. 66:23*	*Heb. 12:28*
Ps. 95:1, 2, 6–9	*Hab. 2:20*	*Rev. 14:7*
Ps. 96:9	*Matt. 4:9, 10*	*Rev. 15:4*

PRAYER JOURNAL

Use these pages to record your own passionate prayers.
Include texts or quotations that have been meaningful to you.
Make a list of prayer requests. Note the date you begin
praying for someone or something as well as the date your
prayer is answered. You will be amazed to see how God
works in your life and in the lives of those for whom you pray!

PASSIONATE PRAYER PROMISES